MN

WI

MI

IA

IL

IN

OH

MO

KY

AR

TN

MS

AL

GA

LA

FL

NY

APPALACHIAN MOUNTAINS

Mount Katahdin

Champlain Mountain

ME

Tumbledown Mountain

VT

NEW ENGLAND

Mount Madison

Franconia-Pinkham Notch

Mount Horrid

NH

Algonquin Peak

Mount Monadnock

Mohonk Preserve

Mount Everett

MA

RI

Bear Mountain

Talcott Mountain

CT

Loyalsock Trail

Black Forest Trail

PA

NJ

Youghiogheny Loop

MD

DC

DE

Dolly Sods

Seneca Rocks

WV

Old Rag Mountain

Endless Wall

Calvary Rocks

VA

Red River Gorge

NC

Linville Gorge

Great Smoky Mountains

SC

Little River Canyon

AMERICA'S GREAT
MOUNTAIN
TRAILS

TERRAIN ELEVATION

8,000 feet

6,000 feet

4,000 feet

2,000 feet

1,000 feet

500 feet

Miles

0   200

La Coca Trail

PR

AMERICA'S GREAT
MOUNTAIN TRAILS

AMERICA'S GREAT
MOUNTAIN TRAILS

100 HIGHCOUNTRY HIKES OF A LIFETIME

Text and Photographs by
TIM PALMER

Foreword by JAMIE WILLIAMS

RIZZOLI
NEW YORK

New York · Paris · London · Milan

Contents

Foreword

AS WITH MANY OTHER PEOPLE, my connection to mountains and wild places goes way back. My friends and I explored the hills and rivers where I grew up, and we still recount both the great adventures and quiet escapes we shared. Later, when I first saw big mountains, they called to me like a gravitational force. As soon as I was old enough, I coaxed my parents to send me off to the Colorado Outward Bound School and later the National Outdoor Leadership School, where, in another few years, I ended up teaching in the mountains of Wyoming and Montana and sharing my growing passion with others. All of this, and more, led irrevocably to a career in conservation.

Mountain trails don't send everybody on the path of their life's work, as they did for me and for author and photographer Tim Palmer, but they do launch those who are open to mountain magic on a path to somewhere meaningful, if not momentous. Mountain trails are the way we get to know both beautiful places and also ourselves. They are the way we get to know that beautiful places *exist*. There's nothing like going there and taking a deep breath of wildness to really register the message: we all need what mountains have to offer. They move and restore our spirits. They inspire us in ways we might never have imagined. They serve the ecology of larger landscapes with their rain-collecting headwaters and forests. Knowing special places is how we start to care about them and how we ultimately engage in decisions that affect them into the future.

Given my own personal journey, and the work I pursue every day of my life, I can't tell you how much I enjoyed this book. Tim has scored a bull's-eye with his obvious goal of creating a state-of-the-art reference book that doubles as a stunning photo documentary of the nation's finest mountain strongholds. Offering both an inspirational narrative and practical details, he explains how we can all absorb the essential spirit of these places. But his effort subtly reaches far beyond that. He celebrates what's best about America, and his infectious enthusiasm will lead others to not only experience these rugged wilds, but also connect in greater ways to the wonder of irreplaceable landscapes: from Acadia National Park in New England to the Lost Coast of California, from endangered wildlife refuges in Alaska to the tropical island of Puerto Rico.

Tim also makes it clear that no one has to travel to the ends of the earth to benefit from the gifts mountains offer. For many, intriguing attractions await not far from home. A lot of driving or flying is not required. As our guide to the nation, Tim shows the way with this premier selection of destinations that will whet our appetites for more, including local pathways that we might discover—all by ourselves—not far from our own back doors.

I'm privileged to work full time for the protection of these and other wild places all across America. For future generations, I'm honored to strive to safeguard the destinations that this book reveals. To preserve these places intact is worth whatever is required. There's no better evidence of this than Tim's collection of mountain trails—and the adventurous opportunities they present—on the pages that follow.

JAMIE WILLIAMS
President and Executive Director, The Wilderness Society

The Flat Tops Wilderness rises east of Trappers Lake in Colorado.

Into the Mountains

AMERICA'S MOUNTAIN RANGES OFFER pathways to both high adventure and calming serenity, and mountain trails take us to remarkable places seen in no other way. The mere image of rugged terrain can stir our imagination, our sense of wonder, and our yearning for authentic physical experience. Some of America's greatest mountain trails are legendary, and some are scarcely known, but all can appeal to people seeking connection to nature and a change of pace from ordinary routines.

It's no wonder that mountains are favorite destinations for one-day escapes, summer vacations, and extended expeditions. Since the earliest days of leisure in America, people have journeyed to retreats in New York's Adirondack Mountains. On the West Coast, John Muir—America's first prominent wilderness advocate—blazed paths into the Sierra Nevada that millions now follow. Modern travelers venture to harsh summits in the desert and bold peaks in the Far North. The most beloved national parks are literally made of mountains, from the abrupt rise of Acadia's headlands in Maine to the sultry blue ridges of the Great Smoky Mountains in Tennessee, and from the Rockies behind Denver's skyline to the colossal dome of Mount Rainier looming icebound over Seattle.

America's Great Mountain Trails will introduce readers to 100 hikes of a lifetime and provide the information needed to plan trips to each. Outings range from very easy to very hard. Some tread not far from roadsides; others lie so remote that few people will ever be able to go there. But for many of the hikes, I've focused on fabulous mountain destinations that might be readily reached without a lot of driving and that are safe for most people.

My selection treads a variable line, including must-see attractions and sometimes offering alternate paths that are magnificent but less used. So often the extremely beautiful trails are also immensely popular. Many of the most-sought landscapes require permits, acquired in advance, in order to ameliorate the perils of crowding. I also mention other hikes nearby in case you want something shorter, or longer, or if you have to switch to Plan B for whatever reason. Conspicuously absent here are America's most famous long-distance trails—the Appalachian, Pacific Crest, Continental Divide, and a few others. These have been written about elsewhere, though I've cherry-picked some sections of these renowned footpaths for their exceptional rewards.

I've personally hiked on all 100 of the trails featured here. Keep in mind that my trips occurred under all types of conditions, but mostly good ones, and a casual stroll can turn into a challenging and potentially dangerous episode with a quick switch of the weather, an unfortunate turn from the intended route, or a surprise slip on snow, ice, or rock—all of which can happen to the freshest novice or the most experienced veteran. Mountain hiking, by its very nature, involves negotiating the unknown. But the uncertainty makes every trip not only eye-opening, but also adventurous, fun, and memorable.

Some hikers might question the wisdom of promoting special places that are already heavily used. Yet everyone deserves an opportunity to be emotionally moved by nature's most appealing gems, and, in the end, protecting the natural world depends on everyone being inspired to do so. The greater danger we face is not that too many people will love and visit these refuges, but that not enough people will know them and thus be moved to sustain them. This takes us to an important pathway after the hike is over: engaging in the defense of your favorite place can be just as rewarding as going there and even more satisfying in critical ways.

Mountains elevate our spirits with their grand beauty, their promise of something exceptional, and their height. We need our mountains, and this book was created so we might know them better. But before we lace up our boots or sneakers, I'd like to share a preview of the wonders that await, a view to what makes mountains so important, and a few thoughts about essential preparations and safety.

Cucumber Falls sprays elegantly downward near the Youghiogheny River in Pennsylvania's Ohiopyle State Park.
FOLLOWING SPREAD: The sun sets north of Washington's Mount Baker.

PART I

THE MOUNTAINOUS HEART OF AMERICA

The Wonders
of Rugged Terrain

BRILLIANT CLUSTERS OF PAINTBRUSH, penstemon, and cinquefoil bloomed in blue, red, and yellow alongside the Highline Trail of Glacier National Park in Montana. The vivid garden ended abruptly in a grove of wind-sculpted fir, resinous with lemony scent and chilled with morning downdraft at 7,000 feet above sea level. I drew a crisp breath into my lungs, partly because I needed an extra dose of oxygen at the high elevation, partly because the air smelled so good, and partly because I felt so free and light-headed that I just wanted more, more. Simply being in that place, and breathing, made me feel good.

The morning sun added its golden rays to the mountain freshness evident everywhere. It shone bright in meadows, though its warming effect was buffered by a breeze sweeping down from an open refrigerator of night-chilled rock that loomed above. Beaming on dew and frost, the light reflected and glowed, dazzling my eyes as if everything had been given a new coat of nature's colors just an hour before dawn. My world was not just illumined by light, but by *mountain* light.

Water—the essential ingredient for life—appeared everywhere. I could see it, hear it, smell it, feel it. Water had been sponged up in moss and the mattress roots of heather. It beaded like glassy prisms on the blue petals of gentians and trickled from spring seeps on cliff walls. It showered down from waterfalls sourced in lingering drifts of snow. As it collided with rocks blackened by lichen, it sprayed in a billion drops like Fourth of July sparklers arcing out through space and then coalescing into rivulets, creeks, and, ultimately, brawling rivers somewhere far downstream.

Above me rose a dramatic line of summits. The Livingston Range bladed the sky and stretched toward Canada. Sharp ridges etched their

Two families explore the delights of the Highline Trail
in Glacier National Park in Montana.

profiles with astonishing clarity given the enormity of the scene and the horizon's great distance. The peaks were topped with broken rock that from miles away looked like mounds of sifted flour, and below them the glaciers had chomped huge bites, leaving jagged northern slopes that tumbled down to rock rubble and a pioneering forest below.

On this morning outing I was not alone. With dark shining eyes, a fluffy fleece of white, and an unalarmed and seemingly wise disposition, a mountain goat stood sentinel on a rock outcrop just above me. The peaceable, athletic ungulate ranks as one of the ultimate mountain creatures, with its thick insulation for winter storms, hooves outfitted in soft soles, two flexible toes for supertraction, and a stomach that craves native forbs and grasses. I don't know what the goat really saw, but his eyes seemed to be set on the same panorama that I admired, as if the scenery were the topic of an unspoken conversation between us.

The trail contoured across a steep slope that veered up on my right and down on my left. I enjoyed a perspective that only comes with elevation. I didn't just look *out* to the rest of the world; I also looked *down* on it—thousands of feet to whole worlds of forests, streams, rivers, hills, and lakes. Then I gazed upward to crags that disappeared into the clouds. I liked what I saw below, but was irresistibly drawn toward the heights capped by resistant sandstone and toothed with fearsome canines at the rocky spine of the continent.

At an opportune spot I began to scramble upward. Steep as a stairway but grassy with wildflowers, my route pulled me in a heart-thumping, lung-puffing ascent. Where the slope angled even sharper, rocks took over—a talus slope of broken shale with thousands of flattened but cleanly cleaved shards, as if the Library of Congress had dumped all its books here long ago and then each one became petrified. Above the olive-colored, lichen-coated talus, larger rocks dominated. Carefully I stepped from one to another. Every 10th rock or so tipped slightly under my weight with the gritting crunch of pulverized minerals.

Up and up I climbed until at last I approached a knife-edge ridge where only the sky rose above me. With one final step—the step that motivates people to climb whole mountains—a new world burst upon me, and the view to the other side and its dizzying free fall took my breath away.

The maroon cliffs where I perched angled straight down until they disappeared into a sinister-looking cavity called a bergschrund, where glacial ice, in summer, pulls away from the rock, leaving a black gap of frightening empty space. Downward from there the snowy surface of the glacier rumpled across a steep slope with a chaos of crevasses and onward to lower fell-fields of finer rock. These continued to lakes and evergreen slopes, then to more drops beyond the gravel piles of ancient glacial moraines, and finally to pinelands that paraded eastward until they melded seamlessly into the shortgrass prairie of the Great Plains.

I had climbed to the top of the continent. The steep ridge where I stood split the prevailing winds' apportionment of snow and rain; behind me now, to the west, water flowed into McDonald Creek, then the Flathead River, the Columbia River, and the Pacific Ocean. Before me, to the east, water trickled down to Swiftcurrent Creek, the Saint Mary River, the Milk River, the Missouri, the Mississippi, and ultimately the Gulf of Mexico and Atlantic Ocean. I ate my lunch there at the divide, looking down and thinking about mountains and all their possibilities for discovery and adventure.

That morning hike in Montana took me to a cherished place that I now regard as a starting point. Beyond it, a thousand miles of Rocky Mountain peaks and valleys stretched southward. To the west, and also to the east, 10 other magnificent ranges rose to dominate the skylines of the continent. During the next few years, camera in hand, I traveled to all of them, searching for the most outstanding mountain trails in America.

A bighorn sheep grazes at the edge of highcountry forests along the Grinnell Glacier Trail in Montana.

The Meaning of Mountains

ENCOUNTERS WITH REALLY BIG MOUNTAINS typically occur during summer vacations, on winter ski trips, or through extended hiking expeditions, but mountains are a part of everyday life, whether in the farmed valleys of the Appalachians or within view of Mount Baldy in Los Angeles. Even if you can't see mountains from where you live, they're important. They touch us all.

While looking out at a climb ahead, I once wondered what a completely flat America would be like. The Coastal Plain where Captain John Smith landed his sailboat in Virginia would continue westward, uninterrupted by the Appalachians. This forever tabletop would drone across the Midwest the whole way to the Pacific Ocean without the Rockies, the Sierra Nevada, or the headlands now enshrined as California's coast. A flat America wouldn't *be* America, but a whole nation of swampy Floridas, or maybe a big Western Hemisphere Bangladesh.

Instead, mountains and their foothills roughen the surface of 40 percent of the United States. Except for the Atlantic seaboard and vast mileage of the Midwest and Great Plains, plus lesser pockets of flatness here and there, mountains or their remnant hills corrugate the continent. West of the Great Plains, summits edge the skyline virtually everywhere. Mountains are what make America what it is, and they make much of life as we know it possible in fundamental ways.

For example, along with prevailing winds, mountains govern the climate. They force the air up, cooling it three to five degrees for every thousand feet of rise, which results in rain and deep snow in highcountry because cooler air cannot hold water vapor as well. Western forests grow in mountain terrain because that's where rain and snow fall the most. Rain shadows or dry belts occur on the leeward side of many western

The startling blue of Marie Lake contrasts with the granite landscape of the upper San Joaquin basin in the Sierra Nevada of California.

ranges, where the air coasts down once again to warmer elevations and retains its water vapor until the next uplift is encountered.

Mountains of the West are the source of 90 percent of the water in the region. Virtually every city supply and irrigation system depends on snowmelt, rain, and related groundwater seeping down from above. In Colorado, alpine highcountry alone produces 20 percent of the state's streamflow, though that photogenic topography accounts for less than four percent of the land. In the East, the Appalachians contribute a disproportionate share of water to the greater region. Runoff from the Catskill Mountains provides for the sinks and tubs of New York City. The mountains might be crudely regarded as a water machine for towns and farms that couldn't exist without the high slopes, however distant, that collect the snow and rain and deliver them to the rivers that feed canals, pipelines, and spigots.

As basic to life as water, soil also comes from mountains. While the rocks at high elevations impart a comforting feel of permanence and a Gibraltar sense of stability, in the test of time they are weaker than water. Grain by grain, stone by stone, rocks erode under the forces of ice, runoff, and wind, which redeposit the pulverized minerals as soil in valleys, on lowlands hundreds of miles downwind, and on floodplains fingering the whole way to the oceans. The fertile dirt of the East Coast's Piedmont lowlands didn't just happen overnight; through the eons it washed off the Appalachians or weathered from chemical decomposition of the foothills. Alluvium in California's Central Valley accumulated to an astonishing depth of 20,000 feet, all eroded from the Sierra Nevada and Coast Range. The fertile soil of the Snake River Plain, which grows Idaho's famous potatoes, blew in from glaciated highlands until the wind lost its grip and the dirt from distant mountain sources settled as thick brown piles of loess.

Water-rich and nourishing mountains also offer a splendid succession of habitats. As elevation increases, lowland plant species yield to mid-elevation forests and on up to alpine forbs, flowers, and lichens. Adding more variety, slopes vary in aspect from south-facing warmth to cool northern exposures. All these features create ecological niches for distinctive forms of life. Mountain goats at the Continental Divide, for example, are a species adapted to gradient, rock, and snow, and other creatures also respond with the savvy to linger year-round. The tiny pika lounges through winter hours in rock piles eating grass it harvested all summer and then cached underground. Some species just sleep through the coldest months. The groundhog-like marmot is the largest true hibernator (bears awake now and then in winter). Deer and elk spend winter at low elevations, but eagerly migrate higher with the advancing springtime, which progresses upslope 100 vertical feet per day with fresh growing forbs. Bighorn sheep do likewise, though at higher levels. Even at lower elevations, fish—including trout, steelhead, and salmon—require cold water that is sourced up above.

Owing to their rugged terrain, mountains have been developed far less than flatter land. Some cities appear at the edge of mountains, but not within them. Where mountain towns occur, they tend to be small and tucked into valleys. Because more of nature survives in the mountains, wildlife finds its ultimate refuge there. Elk once grazed heartily on the Great Plains, but retreated to the safety of mountain enclaves when faced with the sodbusters. Grizzly bears once ruled the lowlands, pawing at salmon along San Francisco Bay and at prairie dogs in Kansas, but as they were shot off and had their habitat usurped, they were consigned to remote mountain sanctuaries in just one percent of the country. When biologists reintroduced gray wolves to the West in 1995, they chose the remote mountains of Yellowstone National Park as the best place to give the howling canines an opportunity to reinstate an ancient and necessary balance in the food chain.

Crevasses caused by underlying rock structure streak the glaciers' white veneer on the northern face of Mount Baker in Washington.

Like the wild animals that retreated to the mountains in order to survive, people who mostly live on flatter land now turn to higher country for recreation and escape. The American Hiking Society reported that 43 million people per year go hiking. Forest Service data indicates that even more people use trails of all kinds. Whether the destination is a lake nestled beneath snowy peaks, a footpath through midslope forests, or a cabin in an Appalachian hollow, mountain retreats meet a whole suite of modern needs.

People come to the mountains for adventure, scenery, and a change of pace, but also for peace, tranquility, and a spiritual bonding with the earth. Mountains are holy places in virtually every religion and culture, likely going back to the birth of humankind. The Greek gods lived on Olympus. According to scripture, Moses received the Ten Commandments on Mount Sinai. Jesus imparted his best-known lessons in the Sermon on the Mount. American Indians hold the San Francisco Peaks, Mount Rainier, and scores of other summits—most, in fact—as sacred.

Clouds swirl at mountaintops, which bridge the earth with the heavens and connect multiple worlds: the flat and the vertical, the backyard and the wilderness, the normal and the extraordinary. Mountains draw us to come, to see, and to appreciate what they mean to all of life. Yet they are not exempt from the forces that threaten nature, wildness, and beauty everywhere.

While people love mountains, these landscapes stand at the front line of damage in an age of environmental crisis. The most severe threats come from mining, including the scourge of mountaintop removal and strip mining. The most ironic challenges stem from people's desire to build homes and resorts for the enjoyment of mountains. Suburbanization through ski resorts, second-home havens, and urban sprawl creeping upslope from nearby cities all raise the difficult question: How can we protect the values that attract people to mountains in the first place? And the most pervasive threat to mountain habitat is now global warming, with dramatic reductions in snowpacks and glaciers, warmed and depleted water supplies, habitat loss, desiccating droughts, intensified storms and fires, rising floods, and invasion of exotic species, including disease-carrying insects. A twofold response to climate change requires a reduction in the burning of fossil fuels—the chief cause of the problem—and enhanced resilience of mountain landscapes. This can be done by reserving floodplains for increasingly high water, zoning to prevent development in the most fire-prone areas, and establishment of open-space corridors for wildlife migration between lowlands and highcountry.

While many of the hikes in this book lie within landscapes protected as national parks, wilderness areas, or state parks, some of them do not,

OPPOSITE: Oaks, hickories, maples, and a young Fraser magnolia shade the flanks of Old Rag Mountain and brighten the October scene with autumn color.
A mountain goat gazes at the view along the Highline Trail in Glacier National Park in Montana.

and they remain vulnerable to modern threats. Even the remotest and best-protected enclaves are subject to global influences of air pollution and climate change. One way or another, most of America's mountains are in jeopardy. Yet compared to elsewhere, they remain as refuges from worse conditions down below, and that makes the care of these landscapes especially important. To address today's problems, people and citizen organizations in every range are working toward a better future that recognizes the value of these extraordinary places.

Among all the strategies for protection, wilderness designation offers the best chance to sustain America as it existed before highways, dams, mowed lawns, and power lines. Applying only to land already owned by the federal government, congressional designation of wilderness means that no logging, roads, or development will occur. Only five percent of America has been protected as wilderness, mostly in high mountain areas. Alaska accounts for the largest share; only two percent of the Lower 48 states is enrolled. Another 58 million acres of federal land outside Alaska are safeguarded as "roadless" by an administrative ruling in 2001, though this status has been threatened by congressional or administrative repeal.

Perhaps a reform-minded Congress in the future will take long-overdue action to rescind America's most damaging mining statute, as dated as its name suggests: the Mining Law of 1872. With increased citizen engagement in the years to come, perhaps land development throughout the mountains will better follow the logic of sound planning. And hopefully this country will come to grips with climate change by reducing the use of fossil fuel and enhancing resilience in every ecosystem.

America's finest mountains deserve protection that honors their contribution as the source of water and soil, the fundament of life, and the refuge for all who venture out to the beauty of mountain trails across this country.

An impending October snowstorm builds at
sunset north of Mount Baker in Washington.

Before the Adventure Begins

HIKING IN THE MOUNTAINS IS FUN, but it also requires attention to safety and logistics, so before you head off into the highcountry, let's discuss possible hazards and tips for planning a mountain adventure. The information in this book is offered as accurately as possible, but be aware that conditions change, varying sources sometimes disagree, mistakes can be made, and parameters of safe travel vary with the individual, the season, the weather, and more.

All hikers must, of course, assume responsibility for their own safety and make their own accurate personal assessment of hazards. That's part of the fun and adventure! Along with the stunning scenery, vigorous exercise, and good company, personally facing hazards with competence is one practice that makes mountain hiking more exciting and interesting than, say, strolling on the sidewalk or, for that matter, sitting on the couch—which may, in the long run, be a more dangerous habit than hiking in difficult terrain.

Regardless of anything a guidebook or advisor says, hikers need to know their own limitations, the conditions of the trail, and the weather forecast at the time of their outing. Because readers represent a wide range of abilities, the information on these pages should not be taken as a recommendation for any particular person to set off on any of these trails. In other words, this information is no substitute for common sense, prudence, experience, fitness, training, skill, adequate equipment, safe weather conditions, and competent personal assessment of dangers.

A survey by the National Park Service found that the most frequent causes of hiking accidents are not bears or avalanches, but lack of knowledge and poor judgment. Every hiker needs the requisite level of fitness and knowledge to safely enjoy their chosen trail, and nothing substitutes for

The trail to Grinnell Glacier climbs toward the Rocky Mountain crest in Glacier National Park in Montana.

experience that builds incrementally to the challenges at hand. Avoiding dangerous situations is far more effective than coping with problems after they arise. Beginners should start with easy outings. Consider joining an organization that offers training and carpooling to trailheads or team up with experienced partners. All hikers must be properly equipped, but no one needs to be a gear geek. Adequate footwear, warm garb, and rain protection are essential. For overnight backpacking, additional gear is required, but it doesn't have to be new, fancy, or expensive.

Map reading is an essential skill for most hikes and all extended trips, and a map will be desired, if not needed, for many of the outings described here. Beware of dependency on smartphones and GPS devices that may not have service in remote locations or may otherwise fail for reasons as common as a dead battery. If a map and compass are not your primary means of navigation, they should always be available as a backup. U.S. Geological Survey topographic maps were once the standard, but hikers can now buy maps especially tailored to many popular destinations at outdoor stores and online. National forest maps cover larger areas and may be adequate for hikes when detailed topo isn't needed.

Drinking adequate amounts of water is essential. Dehydration may be the most common problem that hikers face, and drinking water helps reduce the effects of altitude sickness and fatigue. While untouched high water sources may be safe, most are not pristine or high enough to guarantee purity. Virtually all surface sources could be affected by giardia spread by mammals, and authorities recommend filtering or treating all drinking water. Investigate techniques and ask for advice at your local outdoor store. I've used filters of several kinds and ultraviolet-light purifiers. Carry enough water to last until you reach the next source; I always haul at least a quart, and when backpacking I drink heavily when I come to a good stream that I can purify.

Afternoon thunderstorms, like the one brewing here at Independence Pass in Colorado, pose dangers to hikers above timberline. On many days, and especially in the Rocky Mountains in summer, hikers should plan to be off the summits and ridgelines before noon.

Not to alarm anyone unnecessarily, but other dangers include lightning, altitude sickness, hypothermia, stream crossings, steep snowbanks, rockfall, avalanches, cornices, getting lost, and, in rare cases, wildlife. Learn about these hazards if you're doing any serious hiking in the mountains. I recommend *Mountaineering: The Freedom of the Hills*—written for climbers but also good for hikers—and *The Backpacker's Field Manual* by Rick Curtis.

Hikers also need to be attuned to their own effects on fragile landscapes. Never shortcut trails between switchbacks; this aggravates erosion by water and creates serious maintenance problems. Avoid sensitive ground such as wetlands, damp meadows, and the desert's lichen-filled cryptogamic soil, easily identified by its dark, upraised, and textured crust. Instead, walk in the desert's water-eroded washes, step rock to rock, or avoid cryptogamic areas. Bury human waste far from water sources or camping spots—200 feet or more is recommended. In well-used areas, pack out toilet paper in a plastic bag; it's not as troublesome as it may sound. Contain and minimize the scars of campfires, or don't build them and use a camp stove instead. Respect others and wildlife by being quiet. Don't harass animals by approaching so close that they alter their behavior, even for that special photo you'd love to get. Read Leave No Trace guidelines and follow them.

Unfortunately, hiking is no longer free everywhere; in order to manage recreation use properly, federal or state agencies often require permits. While national and state parks have long charged entrance fees even for single-day use, some national forests now do so in the form of parking permits. It's best to check online or by phone with the administering agency wherever you plan to go. (Seniors who are 62 or older are eligible for a Lifetime Senior Pass good for most federal sites.) Apart from entrance fees to the parks, most day hikes covered in this book can be done without a permit, though some of the more popular summit climbs require one. Permits are needed for many of the overnight trips, especially in national parks. The most visited of these are rationed to limited numbers of hikers. Check online or by phone, and apply for your permit well ahead of time—sometimes a whole year in advance.

For many hikers, long trips by car or plane are not necessary to launch a fabulous walk in the mountains, and travel to distant destinations abroad is certainly not needed. To minimize your carbon and fossil-fuel footprint, hiking in a range near home is a great option, and scheduling long hikes that last for days or weeks at a time eliminates the need for daily driving. In this way, make the best use of the gas you burn. Take public transit when possible. This book's enticement to travel by foot is not intended to encourage more driving, but rather less of it in your planning and enjoyment of free time.

In springtime or even in winter, the Appalachian, West Coast, and Desert Ranges can open up beautifully for hiking. In higher ranges—including the Rockies, Sierra Nevada, Cascades, and Alaska Ranges—hiking in early summer can be rewarding, with blooming wildflowers, snow-capped peaks, and vigorously bubbling streams, but mountain travel then has its challenges. Lingering snow might obscure the trails' routes. Streams rush swiftly and sometimes dangerously at crossings, and bugs can be maddening. After midsummer, these problems wane. The highcountry and northern ranges appeal especially from midsummer through early autumn. The number of hikers everywhere diminishes sharply after September 1, which can be a big plus. Splendid weather often lingers into October if one prepares for cool nights. My favorite season in most mountains is early autumn. Even in winter's snowy months, hearty hikers can enjoy low-elevation walks or ski or snowshoe on many of the trails described here.

At any time of year, use common sense and prudence in the selection and planning of your hike, and then step onto your mountain trail with joy and anticipation for the great adventure to come.

Backcountry skier Ryland Gardner approaches Granite Creek and its narrow snowbridge in Wyoming's Grand Teton National Park.
FOLLOWING SPREAD: Afternoon shadows deepen near Piegan Pass in Glacier National Park in Montana.

PART II

100
MOUNTAIN
TRAILS
OF A
LIFETIME

NEW ENGLAND

Eleven major mountain ranges and hundreds of subranges define the shape of America, and each offers its own world of wonders. Eldest among them, the ancient Appalachians became worn down long before the western uplifts even existed, and, in northern reaches, the mountains of New England and New York—artistically shaped by continental glaciers—showcase some of the finest Appalachian terrain.

Weather-resistant granite caps high profiles of the northern mountains while lower ridges and gentler summits surround the quintessential New England farms and villages tucked into lower slopes across six states.

The Longfellow Mountains of Maine are crowned by a prominent monolith—Katahdin—the only eastern peak that matches the bedrock exposure of a glacier-carved landmark in the West. Southward from there, New Hampshire's White Mountains soar high with forests, tumbling brooks, and meadows perched breathlessly above timberline. Here Mount Washington tops off the Northeast at 6,288 feet. The Green Mountains of Vermont relax a bit in profile with red spruce lingering from a cooler postglacial era on wooded summits. In Massachusetts, the Berkshires' shapely terrain rumples down into Connecticut with the Taconic Mountains bordering New York and, farther west, the Adirondacks feature granite heights and boggy depths honed by glaciers. South of them, the picturesque Catskill Mountains inspired a whole culture of early American literature and painting.

The Appalachian Trail runs north-south through New England and southward through the Appalachian chain while hundreds of connectors and tributary trails lace this region. Built by volunteers and largely maintained by hiking clubs, trails of New England include some rock-armored sections ranking among the steepest and most rugged in America. While most hikers hit these paths in summer, springtime beckons in lower terrain and autumn dazzles with fall color from late September to November.

Champlain Mountain

LOCATION: Acadia National Park, coast of Maine

LENGTH: 4 miles out and back, or 5 miles point to point

ELEVATION: 1,058 feet at top; 100 feet at Bear Brook Trailhead

DIFFICULTY: strenuous but short

HIGHLIGHTS: cliffs, northern forest, vigorous climb, ocean views

This is the home of Acadia National Park—a scenic highlight of the East—and on this hike, wind-sculpted pines and white-barked birches frame scenes of the Atlantic Ocean and mountaintops scraped bare by ice once covering the park's expanse across Mount Desert Island. Champlain ranks as the tallest mountain rising directly from the Atlantic coast in the United States—1,000 feet up from the sea. This trail climbs the northern ridge through stunted conifers and hardwoods, weaves among granite boulders, traverses bedrock that traps vernal pools, and emerges with views to the ocean and its Porcupine Islands.

On clear days, seeing the sun rise over the Atlantic is a bonus on this mountain. Tempting as it may be to catch America's earliest light from a sleeping bag, backpack camping is not allowed in Acadia. So, for the best show, embark on this hike an hour before dawn.

From Champlain's summit, one trail connects to adjacent Cadillac Mountain; another entices hikers south to Gorham Mountain and Otter Cliff. Throughout, mosquitoes and blackflies are troublesome early in summer, less so after June. The later you go, the better.

From Bar Harbor, drive on Route 3 south and then take the Park Loop Road east 1 mile to the Bear Brook Trailhead on the right.

Westward, and beyond the intervening Dorr Mountain, the 1,530-foot Cadillac Mountain rises higher than Champlain, entitling it the earliest sunrise in the United States. But a busy road curves to its top, while Champlain is reached only by foot and overlooks the sea more directly.

Among Acadia National Park's 158 miles of trails, another excellent route tops rocky domes of The Bubbles with views to glaciated terrain all around.

PREVIOUS SPREAD: Mount Katahdin looms over Sandy Stream Pond in Maine's Baxter State Park.

From Champlain Mountain, a view opens to a cloudy sunrise over the Atlantic Ocean in Acadia National Park.

Mount Katahdin

LOCATION: Baxter State Park, central Maine

LENGTH: 10 miles out and back, with other options

ELEVATION: 5,267 feet at top; 1,400 feet at Roaring Brook Trailhead

DIFFICULTY: very strenuous

HIGHLIGHTS: the East's most extreme mountain summit, alpine exposure, glacial features, brooks, lakes

Katahdin ranks as the highest peak in Maine and the ultimate eastern mountain ascent with its upper mass towering boldly above timberline. Dual summits are connected by the Knife Edge—a bedrock ridge that's not really as narrow as a knife, but it is only 5 to 10 feet wide at places, with steep drops on both sides.

More than any other mountain east of the Rockies, this one has the high, glaciated, rock-strewn severity of peaks otherwise found only in America's western cordillera. Katahdin is also a climax and the northern terminus of the Appalachian Trail's full sojourn, which for thru-hikers typically comes at the autumnal end of a six-month expedition requiring 20-mile days. Deep snow persists here until late spring or early summer, and black-flies can be maddening until July or so, making late summer and fall ideal for this classic climb.

Trailheads lie in the somber spruce and balsam fir of Maine's North Woods. The east-side ascent begins at photogenic Sandy Stream Pond—watch for moose! The trail ramps up alongside Roaring Brook to the rockbound beauty of Chimney Pond and its campground beneath Katahdin's severe rise. From there, the Saddle Trail stairsteps 2,300 vertical feet to the heavens.

Katahdin's weather can be notoriously foul, foiling hikers with summit-clinging clouds and unseasonably chilled winds straight from the Arctic. But on a clear day, the expanse of Maine's forested empire rolls out below. Beware of approaching storms on the mountain's exposed plateau, on the sharp rise of the summit, and on its compelling ridgeline.

The trail loops back down via the Knife Edge and Helon Taylor Trail to Roaring Brook for a

On the eastern slopes of Mount Katahdin, the clean, cold water of Roaring Brook tumbles toward the Penobscot River—a reminder that mountains are the sources of the streams and rivers below.

Chimney Pond reflects the spruce and birch forest beneath the rocky slopes of Katahdin.

OPPOSITE: Katahdin rises from its glaciated plateau, while in the background the Knife Edge ramps down from the summit.

round trip of 10 rigorous miles that seem like more. Alternatively, with a car shuttle, hikers can ascend from the south side's intimidatingly steep and boulder-clogged Abol Trail (if open) and descend to the east. Either way, a trip to the summit and back fills—or overfills—a full day for fit hikers. Expanding this trip to two days by camping at Chimney Pond allows for the beauty to soak in deeper.

From Millinocket, drive 18 miles northwest on the Golden Road to Togue Pond Gate of Baxter State Park and then to Roaring Brook Campground.

The county-sized Baxter State Park has 200 miles of trails and 18 peaks topping 3,000 feet, most of them wooded. Furthermore, this northeastern wilderness gem is bordered by Katahdin Woods and Waters National Monument, established in 2016 through a private donation of 88,000 acres to the National Park Service. With perplexing motives, the governor of Maine and his antifederal contingent at the time opposed protected monument status for this extraordinary gift to the people of Maine and America.

Tumbledown Mountain

MAINE

Tumbledown is a little known but engaging outing to a rocky dome rising from the Mahoosuc Range of west-central Maine. Closer to East Coast cities, it offers a much shorter, easier ascent than Mount Katahdin.

This path with occasional scrambles rises through dark woodlands of spruce and birch, sneaks beneath cliffs, and samples recesses where dwarf forests persist in crevices of granite. Sweet huckleberries add a late-season bonus. A network of six trails through Tumbledown Mountain and adjacent Mount Blue State Park offers additional opportunities, including a spur path to the higher but less picturesque Little Jackson Mountain.

From Highway 2 at Dixfield, take 142 north to Weld and continue onward 2.3 miles. Turn west on Byron Road and go 5.6 miles (past the Brook Trailhead) to the Loop Trailhead on the right.

LOCATION: north of Rumford

LENGTH: 3 miles out and back, with longer options

ELEVATION: 3,090 feet at top; 1,500 feet at Chimney Trailhead

DIFFICULTY: strenuous but short

HIGHLIGHTS: northern forest, boulders, cliffs

OPPOSITE: Dripping in morning mist, thickets of mountain ash, red spruce, Labrador tea, and huckleberries thrive near the top of Tumbledown Mountain.

A red maple at the height of autumn color brightens lichen-covered bedrock along the Tumbledown Mountain Trail.

Mount Madison

LOCATION: White Mountain National Forest southwest of Gorham

LENGTH: 9 miles out and back

ELEVATION: 5,363 feet at top; 1,351 feet at Valley Way Trailhead

DIFFICULTY: strenuous

HIGHLIGHTS: northern forest, rocky summit, mountain views

This monolith of New Hampshire's White Mountains rises above New England's wooded empire as the northernmost of six summits constituting the Presidential Range—the longest and highest expanse above timberline in the East.

The rocky approach to this round but bold Appalachian peak ascends through a shadowy green forest of spruce and birch and onward to thickets stunted by severe winters, then to upper slopes of bedrock boulders, granite slabs, krummholz, and wildflowers, all leading to exhilarating exposure at the ridgeline. Like other northern destinations, the weather might not cooperate, but a summer or autumn outing with clear skies is enthralling when you get it. The Appalachian Trail passes near the summit in its arc through the Presidential Range—a highlight of America's most classic footpath. Views to the companion peaks are exquisite.

Nearby Mount Washington impresses with greater gravitas in height and mass, but it tolerates a cog railway and paved road crowding the summit, along with a suite of buildings and weather station paraphernalia, whereas Madison is just Madison.

From Gorham, drive west on Highway 2. Just beyond Randolph, use the Valley Way Trailhead on the left. Ambitious thru-hikes with road shuttles are possible to nearby peaks and Crawford Notch (Highway 302) and Pinkham Notch (Highway 16) Roads.

A summer rainstorm begins to clear in this view from Mount Madison. By forcing prevailing winds to rise, mountains enhance the climate with rain and snow.

OPPOSITE: Red maple leaves decoratively carpet the bedrock of Snyder Brook along Randolph Path—one of several trails approaching Mount Madison from the north.

Franconia Notch to Pinkham Notch

LOCATION: White Mountain National Forest

LENGTH: 56 miles one way

ELEVATION: 6,288 feet at top; 1,950 feet at Franconia Notch Trailhead

DIFFICULTY: strenuous

HIGHLIGHTS: northern forest, miles above timberline, summit views

For an extended northeastern hike with multiple rigorous climbs and repeatedly spectacular views, this route is hard to beat. Just south of Franconia Notch, the initial push on Liberty Springs Trail veers upward, far steeper than engineered trails typical of western states. Meadows and fell-fields of Mount Lafayette are followed by Mount Garfield and others with continuous mileage above timberline. If storms threaten, even in midsummer, wait!

The trail drops like a rock to the Highway 302 crossing at Crawford Notch and then soars skyward again to mileage above the trees, culminating on 6,288-foot Mount Washington, the highest northeastern peak (but not the highest in the East). Some of America's most severe cold and wind have been recorded here, putting many higher locations to shame.

Topping out on Mount Washington is a climax for many hikers, though the busy road and railroad diminish wildness there. On the eastern flank, the trail plunges down Tuckerman's Ravine to deep forests, emerging at the Appalachian Mountain Club's rustic Pinkham Notch base along Highway 16, with accommodations and food for hungry hikers.

From Plymouth or Lincoln, take Highway 3 north to Franconia Notch State Park. The eastern end of this memorably athletic point-to-point expedition is the Appalachian Mountain Club base north of Jackson.

The scene northward from Mount Crawford's granite outcrop shows the rise of the Presidential Range and the rugged terrain crossed by the hiking route from Franconia Notch to Pinkham Notch.

OPPOSITE: Warm colors linger in late autumn on the White Mountains south of Mount Washington.

Mount Monadnock

LOCATION: Monadnock State Park north of Jaffrey

LENGTH: 4 miles out and back

ELEVATION: 3,165 feet at top; 1,400 feet at trailhead

DIFFICULTY: strenuous but short

HIGHLIGHTS: granite slabs, vigorous climb, view to lowlands

The rocky trail up Mount Monadnock has been worn for two centuries by hikers bound for the southernmost of New England's high peaks.

OPPOSITE: Partly covered by clouds and emerging from southern New Hampshire's lowlands, Mount Monadnock is an outlier and a prelude to New England's larger mountains awaiting to the north.

Geographers call a mountain surrounded by lower terrain a monadnock—used as a proper name for this southernmost of steep New England peaks (another Monadnock Mountain appears in northern Vermont). Bulging 1,800 feet from gentle hills and offering a preview of heights northward, this summit is eminently accessible to Boston and the Atlantic coast, and is cited as one of America's most-climbed mountains. It is best to avoid weekends. The barren top owes in part to fires set by early settlers, including—incredibly—efforts to eradicate wolves.

Northeast of Jaffrey, take Highway 124 northwest to Monadnock State Park's visitor center and climb north on the White Dot Trail. Birch thickets yield to granite slabs and boulders. An extensive trail network diffuses foot traffic but confronts hikers with confusing loops; heading up for the summit and down for the trailhead generally works.

Great Cliff and Mount Horrid

LOCATION: Green Mountain National Forest east of Brandon

LENGTH: 2 miles out and back to Mount Horrid summit, with longer hikes possible

ELEVATION: 3,216 feet at top; 2,178 feet at trailhead

DIFFICULTY: easy

HIGHLIGHTS: northern forest, rocky outcrop, view to Lake Champlain

This short walk on the Long Trail climbs 700 feet to a spur path leading to granite outcrops of Great Cliff and views across Lake Champlain. Continue north for Mount Horrid's wooded summit.

Depending on the year, the cliffs might be closed for peregrine falcon nesting from March to August. The Forest Service also warns of overnight break-ins at the Brandon Gap parking lot.

The famed Long Trail of 272 miles from Massachusetts to Canada follows Vermont's Green Mountain chain both north and south from this location. Most mileage is within forests of birch, maple, beech, and hemlock, with red spruce clinging to ridgetops as a remnant from forest recovery after the last ice age. As America's oldest long-distance hiking path, the Long Trail provided inspiration for founders of the Appalachian Trail, which shares its southernmost 100 miles.

From Highway 30 south of Whiting, take Route 73 east to Brandon and continue onward 8 miles to Brandon Pass. Park on the south side and walk north on the Long Trail.

More remote, in northern Vermont, Mount Mansfield is the state's highest peak at 4,395 feet, with the Green Mountain State's only extended alpine zone above timberline. This popular summit can be reached from trailheads in Underhill State Park, but is wisely closed from April to Memorial Day to protect fragile alpine vegetation.

A stand of mature beech trees survives, for now, on the southern flank of Mount Horrid in the Green Mountains. Through much of the Appalachians, beech bark disease has decimated the older groves of this magnificent keystone species.

OPPOSITE: Great Cliff overlooks Lake Champlain from the heights of the Green Mountains, which are golden with birches, beeches, and maples ablaze in autumn color.

Bear Mountain to Mount Everett

LOCATION: north of Salisbury, Connecticut

LENGTH: 17 miles out and back, with other options

ELEVATION: 2,602 feet at top; 800 feet at trailhead

DIFFICULTY: moderate to strenuous

HIGHLIGHTS: forest, waterfalls, mountain views

Connecticut and Massachusetts lack the prestigious high peaks of their northerly New England neighbors, but the Taconic and Berkshire Mountains near the western border with New York offer streamfronts and scenic views nicely linked by the Appalachian Trail (AT).

Among many alternatives here, an excellent choice with one- or two-day options starts at the Undermountain Trailhead, 4 miles north of Salisbury, Connecticut. Arrive early for parking on weekends, and walk up the forested path where shrub-sized chestnut trees—once the keystone canopy of the entire Appalachian chain but decimated since 1920 by an exotic blight—sprout as plentifully as I've ever seen (unfortunately the fungus still kills them at sapling size). After 1 mile, turn right on Paradise Lane Trail. Go another 1.7 miles to the AT, turn right (northbound), and walk 1 mile down the waterfall-laced, hemlock-lined course of Sages Ravine—a highlight of Connecticut hiking, especially when flows surge in spring or after heavy rain.

The AT fords or rock-steps the ravine, enters Massachusetts, and climbs another 2.5 miles to the rock-ribbed escarpment of Race Mountain, a 2,365-foot airy perch above the broad Housatonic

At high flows following an early autumn rainstorm, Sages Ravine must be forded on the northbound approach to Race Mountain.

OPPOSITE: A highlight of the Appalachian Trail in Connecticut, Sages Ravine collects runoff from Bear Mountain to the south and Race Mountain to the north.

Valley. Turn around for a shorter outing, or continue northbound 2 more miles while the AT dips 800 vertical feet to the head of Race Brook and then climbs again to the broad bedrock of Mount Everett and its stunted summit forest of pines and oaks.

Returning southbound, hike back up beautiful Sages Ravine. At the Paradise Lane turnoff, continue right on the AT and veer upward over crazy-steep fractured rock walls to the top of Bear Mountain. Descend its south side for 0.6 miles, turn left on Undermountain Trail, and return in 2 miles to the parking area.

To reach the Undermountain Trailhead from Salisbury, drive 4 miles north on Route 41 and watch for a sign on the left.

This trip can be varied to optional lengths by car; team up with hiking partners, search online for shuttle services, or hitchhike. Mount Everett can also be reached directly by Mount Everett Road, east of the tiny village of Mount Washington. But the road may not be open, leaving hikers with a respectable climb. Another alternative starts from the southeast at the Race Brook Trailhead off Highway 41 north of the Undermountain Trailhead. This path approaches two waterfalls and in 2 miles meets the AT south of Everett's summit.

At the northwestern corner of Massachusetts, Mount Greylock is the state's highest mountain at 3,489 feet. Notch Road out of North Adams reaches the AT near the summit.

In southwestern Massachusetts, Race Mountain forms a dramatic escarpment above the Housatonic River Valley. Here the Appalachian Trail crosses the broad, rock-plated summit.

Talcott Mountain

LOCATION: Talcott Mountain State Park northwest of Hartford

LENGTH: 3-mile loop

ELEVATION: 950 feet at top; 540 feet at trailhead

DIFFICULTY: easy

HIGHLIGHTS: views of central Connecticut, northern hardwoods

Fog fills the valleys below the popular crest of Talcott Mountain.

OPPOSITE: Amber leaves of beech trees and the brighter yellow leaves of maples color autumn slopes on Talcott Mountain.

Rising alone as a north-south ridge in central Connecticut, the uplift of Talcott Mountain offers pastoral views across the Farmington River Valley and rolling hills of southern New England. This easy stroll lies at Hartford's doorstep.

Heavily traveled state park trails zigzag to the top where historic Heublein Tower rises. The whole 557-acre mountain was slated for subdivision but instead was bought in 1965 and rescued as a state park.

From northwestern Hartford, take Highway 185 west, and 1 mile beyond the Route 178 intersection turn left (southwest) into the park.

Talcott Mountain is incorporated into the 215-mile New England Trail—a linkage of established paths and byways designated as an official national scenic trail in 2009 and running north-south through eastern New England.

Algonquin Peak

New York's vast Adirondack Mountains, 70 by 45 miles in extent but feeling as big as a state, are part of the granitic Canadian Shield rearing up in the path of the Appalachians and usually considered a part of this range. Impervious soils and bedrock scraped clean by continental glaciers hold countless lakes and wetlands, all linked by cascading rivers of amber-blue swamp water.

Algonquin—the second-highest summit here and statewide—offers a panorama among 46 Adirondack peaks. The hike starts in dense forest near Heart Lake and climbs into an alpine zone of stunted spruce, windswept granite, and snow cover starting early and lingering through spring.

From the Heart Lake Trailhead, hike south on Van Hoevenberg Trail, turn right onto Algonquin Peak Trail, and follow the rocky corridor through dense conifers. Stay right to skirt the west side of Wright Peak—at 4,580 feet a tempting 0.8-mile round-trip detour—and continue to the windbattered Algonquin summit overlooking the MacIntyre subrange with views all around. For Iroquois Peak's adjoining summit of 4,843 feet, continue southwest 1.4 more miles out and back.

As on other heights of this ancient exposed range, the weather can be awful. In early November I found a wonderland of ice and wind-crusted snow above timberline, with fearsome conditions but amazing views on the summit. Bugs in this lake- and wetland-rich range are maddening in early summer, leaving autumn as a delightful holiday from woes except for the welcoming challenge of gradient and, in late fall, the chance of getting socked with an early winter storm.

From Lake Placid, drive south on Highway 73 to North Elba, turn south on Heart Lake Road, and

LOCATION: Adirondack Park south of Lake Placid

LENGTH: 8 miles out and back, with longer options possible

ELEVATION: 5,114 feet at top; 2,010 feet at Heart Lake Trailhead

DIFFICULTY: strenuous

HIGHLIGHTS: Adirondack views, krummholz forest

In harsh autumn weather, Algonquin Peak's rounded but exposed summit challenges hikers in the Northeast.

go to the Algonquin Peak Trailhead on the south-east side of Heart Lake, which is as picturesque as it sounds.

The Algonquin route connects to an intricate network of trails among the Adirondack High Peaks south of Lake Placid. Only 4 airline miles to the southeast of Algonquin's summit, Mount Marcy, at 5,344 feet, is the highest peak. It offers a similar view, but with a longer approach across bogs and rocky minefields, for a round trip of two days for many hikers.

Stunted by snow, ice, and cold, spruces are whitened by winter's first chilling storm on Algonquin Peak (top). Encrusted in snow and ice, blasted by wind but still luring hikers onward, the summit of Algonquin Peak lies just ahead for the author's wife, Ann Vileisis, on a cold November outing (bottom).

OPPOSITE: Heart Lake marks the beginning of the climb up Algonquin—the second-loftiest peak among the High Peaks of the Adirondack Range and one of the premier mountain destinations in the East.

Mohonk Preserve

LOCATION: west of New Paltz

LENGTH: 6 miles out and back, with other hikes nearby

ELEVATION: 1,195 feet at top; 800 feet at trailhead

DIFFICULTY: easy

HIGHLIGHTS: pastoral and woodland views, northern hardwoods, cliffs

The Catskills and their southerly neighbor—the less storied but more phonetically challenging Shawangunk Mountains—are gentle Appalachian subranges rising west of the Hudson River south of Albany. Trails here go back to the dawn of recreational hiking in America.

Some 75 miles of easy paths and carriage roads wind through the Mohonk Preserve—private but generously open to the public. Deep hardwood forests shade handsome sandstone cliffs, and trails emerge with panoramas of hills and forests recovering from logging a century or two ago.

The 3-mile Bonticou Crag loop leads to a gleaming white outcrop with pastoral views. This and the Table Rocks Trail are reached via the Spring Farm Trailhead. From New Paltz, drive west on Highway 299, turn right on Springtown Road, then left on Mountain Rest Road. Pass the impressive Mohonk Mountain House, and continue 1 mile. Turn right on Upper 27 Knolls Road, and go a quarter mile to the trailhead.

Within the preserve, a 5-mile-long rock face—a signature feature of the Shawangunks—has long been a world-class rock-climbing destination, now attracting 80,000 cliff climbers a year. Carriage roads below and above allow for views of the climbing routes and the landscape. A cultural and architectural draw in its own right, the one-of-a-kind Mohonk Mountain House was first built in the 1800s as a rambling Victorian resort.

At the Mohonk Preserve, the white bedrock of Bonticou Crag, colored with autumn's huckleberry bushes, offers views to the Shawangunk Mountains and a charmingly pastoral quilt of fields and forests.

OPPOSITE: Green leaves of a wild grapevine brighten a misty forest of hardwoods beneath cliffs in the Mohonk Preserve.

CENTRAL AND SOUTHERN APPALACHIANS

South of New England, the Appalachians may have reached 15,000 feet 300 million years ago, but they've long since softened to rolling green mounds with summits, ridges, and plateaus capped by resistant sandstone and occasionally accented by rocky crowns or balds.

Spanning 1,550 miles in the United States and 2,200 miles altogether from Alabama to Newfoundland, Canada, the full Appalachian range runs northeast-southwest with a width of 200 miles or so.

Imagine a lateral center line down the north-south length of the chain from Pennsylvania to Georgia. To its east, ridges run parallel with almost geometrical perfection, harboring sheltered valleys in between. This is the Ridge and Valley Province, extending from the Hudson River in New York to central Alabama. The broadest valleys of calcium-rich limestone are harrowed by Amish and other farmers, and are increasingly being developed for their beauty and accessibility to East Coast cities. The ridges rise as if somebody pushed a carpet up at one end, causing multiple buckles in its middle, which is a fairly accurate analogy for the tectonic forces once at play. The Blue Ridge Mountains of Virginia, extending through North Carolina, are the boldest of these upward bulges—a monolith whose east side plummets into the Piedmont Province of Appalachian foothills and then down to the Coastal Plain.

Southern Appalachian subranges include the bulky grandeur of the Smoky Mountains, which house a greater diversity of plant life than any other region in America. The Black Mountains adjoin northward, where Mount Mitchell, at 6,684 feet, rears higher than any other eastern summit. All 10 of the Appalachians' loftiest peaks lie in these two subranges, but unlike in the North, where winters are harsh and where glaciers scraped the peaks bare, forests in the South cover even the highest summits.

Now back to the imaginary north-south lateral line down the length of the Appalachians: the geologic essence of the west side is not ridge and valley but rather plateau. However, other than in plan view from overhead in space or on a map, the plateau is rarely evident, as rivers and streams have incised so comprehensively that they obscure the comparatively uniform uplift and westward tilt of the region's metalandscape. Because of the streams' erosion, the terrain seen from the valleys usually looks more like freestanding mountains than its ancestrally uniform uplift.

In the North, New York's share of this remnant plateau undulates from forest to farmed field, glaciated as New England was in the ice ages. Pennsylvania's Allegheny Plateau rises higher and wilder, and the continental glaciers abruptly came to their end here. Southward, shale and coal form cake layers of sedimentary deposit that set the stage for the mid-Appalachians' west-slope fate: an unfortunate sacrifice zone for mining. South of Pennsylvania, a tortuous amalgam of hills and hollows gives West Virginia its raw edge and remote charm. There the bygone boom in coal mining reached its tragic zenith, with thousands of miles of polluted streams, entirely decapitated mountaintops in the western half of the state, and chronic poverty of legendary and intractable proportions, though now softened by tourism where the ruins of nature are less severe. In neighboring Kentucky, the Cumberland Plateau supports a rich forest, though seriously compromised by contour stripping for coal that ravaged many steep slopes. Additional forested plateaus extend into Tennessee and Alabama.

Loyalsock Trail

The Loyalsock Trail offers a week of lively up and down featuring recovering northern hardwoods, 31 waterfalls, and nearly as many forested mountain vistas. The trail touches its namesake, Loyalsock Creek (really a river), only at Worlds End State Park and at the Haystacks near the trail's northeastern end.

Road crossings make trips of varying lengths possible. April and May are good here, with open views before the trees fully leaf out and when the Appalachian spring bursts in extravagant bud and bloom. Even better, September and October bring cool weather and autumn's brilliant colors among northern hardwoods. Following the Loyalsock Trail markers takes hikers on an indirect path, but one that's artfully laid out to visit waterfalls and scenic views while avoiding a ubiquitous dirt-road system through state forest and private land—some of those roads and trail crossings are now scarred by fracking wells drilled for natural gas extraction.

From Montoursville, take Highway 87 north for 10 miles to the obscure but signed trailhead on the right (1 mile before Huntersville Road). For the northeastern end, take Highway 220 north from Laporte for 1 mile and go left on Mead Road for 0.2 miles. For a short hike—or a longer one on a related network of fine interlinking trails—go to Worlds End State Park. From Highway 220 at Laporte, take Route 154 west for 8 miles. For a Loyalsock Trail excursion of a few days, walk south from Worlds End, where leaving a vehicle is safe and easy. Pick up a map of the state park at the park office and a copy of the full trail guide from the Alpine Club of Williamsport.

LOCATION: north of Montoursville

LENGTH: 59 miles one way, with shorter hikes possible

ELEVATION: 1,800 feet at top; 600 feet at southwestern trailhead

DIFFICULTY: moderate to strenuous

HIGHLIGHTS: waterfalls, forest views

PREVIOUS SPREAD: The New River carves the greatest gorge in the East, seen here with ridge-capping sandstone and broadleaf trees dazzling in autumn color along the Endless Wall Trail in West Virginia.

Southbound from Worlds End State Park, Loyalsock Creek winds through the Appalachian Plateau on a misty, rainy day.

FOLLOWING SPREAD: At Worlds End State Park in Pennsylvania, Beth and Taylor Sauder—mother and daughter—explore a magnificent hemlock grove along the Loyalsock Trail (left). While hemlocks darken the background, beech trees highlight Appalachian forests along the Loyalsock Trail (right).

Black Forest Trail

LOCATION: Tiadaghton State Forest near Slate Run

LENGTH: 42-mile loop, with shorter hikes possible

ELEVATION: 2,145 feet at top; 760 feet at Slate Run Trailhead

DIFFICULTY: strenuous

HIGHLIGHTS: northern hardwoods, rocky overlooks, streams

This forested path is an eye-opening tour of the Pennsylvania Wilds—half the size of New Jersey with a state forest nucleus of 2.1 million acres and unexpected wildness spanning the northern core of Penn's Woods. Inspired by trails of the Adirondacks, state forester John Eastlake and ranger Bob Webber created this path in the 1970s out of overgrown routes and new connections that climb and descend constantly for a rigorous week of hiking.

With a rhythm of mountain vistas, the trail loops through woodlands locally known as the Black Forest—indicative of hemlocks deeply shading ravines and north slopes incised into the Allegheny Plateau. Unfortunately, an exotic insect—the hemlock woolly adelgid—has eliminated many of those elegant conifers, and its ravage virtually everywhere in the hemlock's range appears inevitable, at least south of the colder New England. Treatment with insecticides is, for now, the only means of keeping a hemlock remnant alive—a stopgap measure with hopes that biological controls through introduced insect predators to the adelgid will eventually have ecosystem-wide effects.

From the town of Jersey Shore, take Highway 414 north to the village of Slate Run, turn west on Slate Run Road, and drive 0.8 miles to the main trailhead. The path intersects other gravel byways of the state forest network, making trips of many lengths possible.

The Black Forest Trail links with two other notable hiking destinations: the looping 85-mile Susquehannock Trail to the northwest and the West Rim Trail, which traces the edge of Pine Creek's "Grand Canyon" to the north. Other long-distance routes in Pennsylvania include the Mid State Trail running north-south and the Laurel Highlands Trail, which stretches 70 miles from its northern terminus in Conemaugh Gorge near Johnstown southward to Ohiopyle State Park.

Groves of hemlocks shade northern aspects, stream bottoms, and steep slopes of the Black Forest Trail.

Youghiogheny Loop

PENNSYLVANIA

LOCATION: Ohiopyle State Park northeast of Uniontown

LENGTH: 5-mile loop, with longer hikes possible

ELEVATION: 1,250 feet at top; 1,217 feet at Ferncliff Trailhead

DIFFICULTY: easy

HIGHLIGHTS: Youghiogheny River whitewater, waterfalls, mature eastern forest

This stroll tours an outstanding suite of scenic Appalachian charms and—for the effort expended—is one of the most beautiful and interesting hikes in the Appalachians.

Begin in Ferncliff Natural Area, a wooded tract on the inside of a U-shaped bend of the Youghiogheny River directly across from the town of Ohiopyle—home of Pennsylvania's most popular state park. The trail here passes through a splendid variety of hardwoods, white pines, and hemlocks growing to impressive girth once again after protection of this area began in the early 1900s. The path crosses bedrock with visible arm-length tree-fern fossils of the carboniferous era and emerges at the brink of 20-foot Ohiopyle Falls—one of the largest waterfalls in the East by volume of flow.

Reentering the forest, the trail arcs downstream around the 1.7-mile Youghiogheny Loop, with side paths to foaming rapids where kayakers and rafters plunge through the most popular whitewater in the East.

Just below Railroad Rapid, cross a high bridge converted from railroad to foot and bike use—an attraction and bit of a thrill in its own right. Turn immediately left on the Great Gorge Trail, and double back upriver for 2.6 miles, now walking upstream on the opposite side from Ferncliff Natural Area. This former railroad bed leads to tributary Cucumber Creek and its elegant 30-foot falls—dayglow orange with mine acid just 50 years ago but exquisite today, and road accessible from Ohiopyle. A path continues up the shoreline of the Youghiogheny and back to its big falls but on the opposite side from the earlier view. Pedestrian paths then lead upriver and across the Youghiogheny's highway bridge back to the Ferncliff parking lot.

With ice accreting in the super-cooled spray zone of Ohiopyle Falls, the Youghiogheny Loop Trail serves up tantalizing scenes even in winter's frigid grip.

From the Pennsylvania Turnpike's Donegal exit an hour east of Pittsburgh, take Highway 31 east for 2 miles. At Route 711, turn right and go south 10 miles, and then at Route 381 turn left and continue 11 miles to Ohiopyle. Just before the Youghiogheny bridge, at the Wilderness Voyageurs Outfitters store on the left, turn right into the Ferncliff parking lot.

Crowds are drawn to Ohiopyle for the whitewater and footpaths, but also for the abandoned railroad that has been converted to gravel at the heart of a 335-mile continuous car-free trail from Pittsburgh to Washington, DC, called the Great Allegheny Passage and C&O Canal Bikeway—the East's exemplary megaroute for bicycling through mountain terrain. The hike around the Youghiogheny Loop can be reached by pedaling your bike from Pittsburgh or Washington, DC!

An easy trail follows the course of the Youghiogheny River as it bisects Chestnut Ridge in Ohiopyle State Park.

Dolly Sods

LOCATION: Monongahela National Forest west of Petersburg

LENGTH: 1- to 10-mile loop

ELEVATION: 4,700 feet at top; trails drop to 2,500 feet

DIFFICULTY: easy to moderate

HIGHLIGHTS: views, rocks, bogs, rare plants, northern ecosystem

Dolly Sods Wilderness is 32,000 acres of wildness at a high point of the Allegheny Front, precisely where the Ridge and Valley Province of the eastern Appalachians ends and the west-side Appalachian Plateau begins. The lofty refuge is exposed to extreme weather with temperatures that can plunge to single digits even in May, yielding an ecosystem typical of Canadian latitudes. The "sods" were named for damp grasslands underlain by impervious soil and bedrock capping the plateau—one of the Appalachians' most open natural landscapes with bogs and shrubs rather than continuous forests. Drier domes support red spruce typical of the North.

A 47-mile network of paths takes hikers through high meadows, wetlands with pitcher plants and acid-loving shrubs, and spruce groves recovering from the past century's abuse of logging, burning, and even artillery practice by the army. Autumn dazzles with red huckleberry, Labrador tea, and orange willows.

The sods were one of a few eastern areas included in the original Wilderness Act of 1964 before the related Eastern Wilderness Act opened reclaimed wildlands to the prestigious federal program. Acreage was added to Dolly Sods in 1975, barring proposed strip mines, but gas-drilling threats continued; wild acreage remains at risk.

From Petersburg, take Highway 55 west to Hopeville. At Route 4 turn right and go 1 mile, at Forest Road 19 turn left and go 6 miles, and at Forest Road 75 (Dolly Sods Road) turn right and proceed on gravel to the trailheads—including Bear Rocks parking area just before Forest Road 75 angles sharp right and plunges back eastward off the plateau. Walk north to the rocks—an outcrop of gleaming quartzite with wind-blasted conifers and vistas to mountain terrain eastward in the Ridge and Valley Province—or walk east into a network of 20 trails. Take a map and compass for this confusing terrain.

The network of paths through meadows, woods, and bogs of Dolly Sods emerges here at Bear Rocks, where a commanding view through weathered spruces faces out to the Appalachians' Ridge and Valley Province of paralleling mountain crests to the east.

Seneca Rocks

LOCATION: Monongahela National Forest west of Petersburg

LENGTH: 3.4 miles out and back, with other options

ELEVATION: 2,500 feet at top; 1,568 feet at trailhead

DIFFICULTY: easy

HIGHLIGHTS: cliffs, climbing routes, mountain views

Seneca Rocks is the largest sheer-wall rock in the Appalachians and a destination for climbers throughout the East. Here South Peak is the tallest technical (Class 5) rock climb east of the Rockies. The near-vertical quartzite face veers 900 feet above the North Fork South Branch Potomac River.

A trail switchbacks through woodlands to a summit just north of the vertical walls; at the top, scramble out to striking views of the rock face and to mountains and forests beyond. At its base, this trail on the northern side of the rocks connects to a valley trail that leads south to additional climbing routes.

From Petersburg, take Highway 55 west and south to the Forest Service visitor center at the junction of Highways 55 and 28/33.

The tallest sheer vertical face in the East, Seneca Rocks aims skyward from the Appalachian forests surrounding it.

Endless Wall

LOCATION: New River Gorge
National River northeast
of Beckley

LENGTH: 5 miles out and back,
or 3-mile loop with road return

ELEVATION: 1,938 feet at top;
1,770 feet at low point

DIFFICULTY: easy

HIGHLIGHTS: cliffs,
recovering forest, greatest
gorge in the East

This trail clings to cliff tops or follows the base of an extended sandstone wall at the top of steep, wooded slopes that pitch down sharply to the New River. Forming the largest gorge in the East, the New is considered the second-oldest river worldwide, maintaining a route that preceded the Appalachian uplift 300 million years ago. Unlike smaller streams that were truncated and forced to divide eastward and westward by the ascending alignment of the Appalachians' backbone, the antecedent New River was powerful enough to cut through bedrock as the topography arose. From the rim above, boulders periodically avalanched into the river, adding to the challenging rapids that now draw rafters and kayakers to the East's premier big-volume whitewater.

From Highway 19 on the north side of the famously high New River Gorge Bridge, and just north of the Canyon Rim visitor center, turn southeast on Lansing-Edmond Road and drive 1.5 miles to the trailhead. Walk south and east to Diamond Point overlook, continue onward for a total of 2.5 miles to another parking area, and then return. Rock walls draw climbers here. Administered by the National Park Service, the national river area offers 50 miles of trails.

Cliff-top perches on the Endless Wall's sandstone rim overlook the New River as it plunges through the greatest gorge in the East.

OPPOSITE: Radial-patterned leaves of Fraser magnolia shade the understory while hemlocks darken the background at the Endless Wall above New River Gorge.

Old Rag Mountain

LOCATION: Shenandoah National Park

LENGTH: 9-mile loop

ELEVATION: 3,284 feet at top; 880 feet at trailhead

DIFFICULTY: strenuous

HIGHLIGHTS: forest, rocks, boulder scrambling, views

A classic climb of the central Appalachians, Old Rag's alluring path is trekked by tens of thousands of hikers each year—the most popular trail in Shenandoah National Park and the finest mountain ascent within a few hours' drive of Washington, DC. Arrive by 7:00 a.m. for parking on weekends or during autumn color, or choose weekdays, spring, or late autumn.

After 0.8 miles of walking from the parking area (which has a fee) to the trailhead, the path climbs through forest and into rocky terrain. Near the summit, the approach includes scrambles among boulders before emerging with views westward to the Blue Ridge crest. The trail loops clockwise back to the beginning by way of a fabulous hardwood forest with girthy tulip trees, oaks, and maples.

Though the hike is within Shenandoah National Park, which centers on Skyline Drive to the west, access to Old Rag is from the east. Take I-66, then 29 south, then 211 west to Sperryville. Take 522 south for 0.8 miles, turn right on 231, continue 8 miles, and then turn right on 601 and continue 3 miles to the parking lot.

Nearby trails connect to the beautifully diminutive Hughes River and southward to Whiteoak Canyon and its streamside climb past waterfalls to the Blue Ridge crest and Skyline Drive—the East's preeminent scenic mountain highway scribing the ridgelines of 105-mile-long Shenandoah National Park.

As a climax to the most spectacular hike in Shenandoah National Park, Old Rag Mountain's rocky top dominates surrounding forest just west of the Piedmont Province of Appalachian foothills.

Calvary Rocks

VIRGINIA

LOCATION: southern
Shenandoah National Park

LENGTH: 2 miles to Calvary
Rocks and back, or 9.6-mile
loop

ELEVATION: 2,720 feet at
trailhead; 1,600 feet at bottom
of the loop

DIFFICULTY: easy to the
overlook, strenuous for the loop

HIGHLIGHTS: overlook, quartzite
outcrops, forest, stream

From milepost 90 of Shenandoah National Park's Skyline Drive, take the Appalachian Trail north for 0.4 miles and turn left on Riprap Trail. At 0.7 miles from the parking lot, watch for the first rocky overlook, followed at 1 mile by Calvary Rocks jutting up through the woods to the left of the trail with sweeping views westward to Shenandoah Valley. Avoid poison ivy!

Turn this stroll into a vigorous workout by continuing down Riprap Trail to Cold Spring Hollow and its green gorge, 20-foot waterfall, and summertime swimming hole where few others are likely to go. At 3.7 miles from the parking lot, turn left on Wildcat Trail and climb steeply back uphill 2.6 miles to the Appalachian Trail. Turn left and walk 2.8 miles back to the Riprap Trail parking lot.

From the southern reaches of Shenandoah National Park—but north of the Rockfish Gap entrance—drive to Skyline Drive's milepost 90 and the Riprap Trail parking lot (not the nearby Riprap Overlook pullout) and walk north and west.

Near the southern end of Shenandoah National Park, Calvary Rocks faces west to the Appalachians' 100-mile width of washboard terrain in Virginia and West Virginia.

Linville Gorge

LOCATION: Pisgah National Forest southwest of Blowing Rock

LENGTH: 3 to 12 miles one way, or hike out and back

ELEVATION: 3,400 feet at trailhead; 1,300 feet at the low point

DIFFICULTY: strenuous

HIGHLIGHTS: eastern gorge, wild stream

In North Carolina, the eastern front of the Appalachians tilts down from the highest elevations of the entire range to the Piedmont Province of foothill terrain. Streams cascading off this escarpment rank as the steepest in the East. Most are small and lack trails, but Linville Gorge has a rough footpath alongside it. A rare gem, this hike follows a wild Appalachian river for 12 miles without a road or railroad to be seen.

First, Linville Falls is worth a look: on the Blue Ridge Parkway north of Marion, drive south on Highway 221 half a mile and at Route 183 bear left to the busy parking lot.

For the real deal here, continue driving south past the Linville Falls turnoff and in another mile

park at a small left-side pulloff for the Linville Gorge Trail. Hike east, immediately descending 500 feet to river level. Follow this unmarked, sometimes discontinuous trail down the west side of Linville River for 12 miles, clinging to canyonsides and jogging in and out of tributary basins.

Several exit trails climb back up the west side of the gorge to meet the same north-south road—now gravel. This clings near the gorge's rim, where cars can be shuttled to takeouts. The Babel Tower Trail climbs out to the southwest (right) rim 3 miles downstream from the Linville Gorge Trailhead. At 10 miles, the Pinch-In Trail climbs 2,000 feet to the rim and road. Minimize guesswork here with Pisgah National Forest's Linville Gorge Wilderness map.

Hikers follow the Linville Gorge Trail and rock-step to the edge of the cascading waterway.

OPPOSITE: The Linville River carries runoff from the Appalachians' highest escarpment toward the lower hills of the Piedmont Province.

Great Smoky Mountains

LOCATION: Great Smoky Mountains National Park

LENGTH: 50 to 60 miles for a mountain-crest hike, plus other options

ELEVATION: 6,643 feet at Clingmans Dome; 1,800 feet at Cades Cove Trailhead

DIFFICULTY: strenuous

HIGHLIGHTS: old-growth forest, mountain streams, views

Within a day's drive of many eastern cities, Great Smoky Mountains is America's most popular national park. Typical visitors drive through and limit outings to short woodland walks, but longer trails lead to superb forests, waterfalls, and occasional views from ridgelines where the southern Appalachians fade away in ever-lighter shades, hazed by the trees' transpiration and, unfortunately, by pollution from power plants and cities to the west.

For all its mountains, this is more a park of forests than peaks. The Smokies are home to more eastern old-growth trees than any other location except the Adirondack Mountains, where old trees tend to be smaller owing to climatic and soil limitations. The Smokies breed more tree specimens of exceptional size (arboreal "champions") than any other place in America.

Hikes of any length and difficulty can be linked among 850 miles of national park trails. My favorite is a 60-mile backpack route traversing much of the park and cresting the highest peaks— though they are almost entirely forested. From Cades Cove in the northwestern end of the park, ascend the Anthony Creek and Bote Mountain

A cottontail rabbit finds a salad bar of greens along the edge of the Appalachian Trail in the Smoky Mountains.

OPPOSITE: A trans–Smoky Mountains hike emerges at the bald top of Clingmans Dome and its legacy Fraser fir snags spiked above a recovering forest.

Trails for 5 miles to the Appalachian Trail, and then follow it 15 miles northeast to the park's highest point (the third highest in the East)—Clingmans Dome at 6,643 feet. A road also leads to this busy panoramic summit. Snags of Fraser firs here show the effects of exotic insect infestations that, in the 1990s, appeared to be eliminating the rare groves of ice-age forest, but for now—with better controls on air pollution—young firs are surviving again.

Northeast of Clingmans Dome, the Appalachian Trail shares the high, broad ridgeline with a road for 8 miles, then quietly leaves it behind at Newfound Gap. In another 2 miles northeastward, a scenic digression on the Boulevard Trail, clinging to an intersecting ridgeline, can be followed for 5 miles north to Mount Le Conte—the park's third-highest point. Returning 5 miles to the northeast-bound Appalachian Trail, it's 1 mile to the outcrop of Charlies Bunion and another 11 miles to forested Mount Guyot—the park's second-highest mountain at 6,621 feet. A conclusive 8-mile drop ends at the road access on the park's northeast side near Cosby, Tennessee. Other trailheads can be found on all sides of the national park.

Get permits for backpacking. Camping is officially limited to prescribed sites. Beware of rodents at these and other regularly used camps in the Appalachians; hang food in bags separate from your pack or in bear-proof canisters.

OPPOSITE: Ramsey Prong cascades at a woodland waterfall in the northern reaches of Great Smoky Mountains National Park.

Great Smoky Mountains National Park excels with many eastern tree "champions"—the largest of their species. Hemlocks here were once the tallest of their kind but have been decimated by an exotic insect infestation.

Red River Gorge

LOCATION: Daniel Boone National Forest southeast of Lexington

LENGTH: 1 to 12 miles, out and back or loop

ELEVATION: 1,266 feet at top; 850 feet at low point

DIFFICULTY: easy

HIGHLIGHTS: geologic arches

The Red River Gorge has the largest collection of stone arches in the East and the second largest in the nation. Trails lead to geologic curiosities rivaling some of those in Utah's Arches National Park, but without the desert's aridity. In Kentucky, you'll find arches in the woods.

For an outstanding route in the Forest Service's Red River Gorge Geological Area, take the 5-mile round trip to Double Arch with its view to the surrounding forested plateau, starting at a trailhead off Highway 77. Other destinations are the 3-mile round trip to Whittleton Arch in its deep, wooded alcove with a wispy waterfall, reached from a trailhead at the end of Tunnel Ridge Road off Highway 77. The trailhead for Grays Arch, 4 miles round trip, also lies off Tunnel Ridge Road. Some routes can be linked together for a backpacking trip on a road-free 11-mile loop called the Rough Trail. Get the Daniel Boone National Forest map and a Forest Service permit for overnights.

At lower elevations in the geological area, the Red River winds through mature mixed hardwoods in a valley slated for impoundment in the 1970s. That ill-conceived dam was thwarted by a citizen effort that gained political traction with support from Supreme Court Justice William O. Douglas. The Red was permanently protected in 1993 when it was designated a National Wild and Scenic River.

Take Highway 15 southeast of Lexington (Bert T. Combs Mountain Parkway) to Route 77 north, or to other exits for Red River Gorge.

Short trails in Daniel Boone National Forest tour one of the nation's most remarkable collections of natural stone arches. Here Double Arch appears after a 2.5-mile approach.

Little River Canyon

LOCATION: Little River Canyon National Preserve southeast of Fort Payne

LENGTH: 1 mile out and back, with other options

ELEVATION: 1,700 feet at top; 1,100 feet at low point

DIFFICULTY: strenuous but short

HIGHLIGHTS: forested gorge, whitewater, rare plants

This extraordinary wooded gorge is the result of the Little River carving deeply into the Appalachian uplift near the southern terminus of the 2,200-mile-long mountain range.

South of Highway 35, short, steep trails drop into the 600-foot gorge, reached from Routes 275 and 176 along the canyon's west rim. Paths at Little River Falls, Two-Mile, Eberhart Point, and Canyon Mouth Park drop to the bottom where the Little River plunges over rapids. Thickets of rhododendron fill the understory of a lush hardwood forest.

From I-59 at Fort Payne, take Highway 35 east to Route 176 south and go to the downstream section of the national preserve.

The Little River tumbles through its remarkable gorge in northern Alabama.

OPPOSITE: Near the southern limits of the Appalachian Mountain chain, several trails descend to the waterline from the perched rim of Little River Gorge.

ROCKY MOUNTAINS

West of the Appalachians, it's a long way before major mountains appear on the horizon. The Ozark, Ouachita, and Boston Mountains of Missouri and Arkansas are mostly "hills" for the purpose of this volume, as are the Porcupine Mountains of Michigan's Upper Peninsula. The Black Hills of South Dakota ramp higher as a precursor to the Rocky Mountains and, finally, at the western limit of the Great Plains, the largest mountain range in America emerges, its front spanning 1,000 miles from New Mexico to Canada. Another 1,500 miles continue farther north through the Brooks Range of Alaska. Though broken by substantial lower terrain, the mountains' southward extension in Mexico becomes the Sierra Madre Occidental. Up to 450 miles in width in the United States, the Rockies' entire cordillera covers more area than any other mountain chain on earth. Sixty major subranges and additional minor ones are separated by valleys and gaps, some quite wide.

The Rockies began with what geologists call the Laramide Revolution, starting 70 million years ago in seismic uplifts and downwarps. The resulting fault-block complex shows sharp relief, such as the Front Range veering from the Plains in northern Colorado. Snow lingers late on these heights, often delaying hiking until June or July. Then mosquitoes can be maddening until the dry-up and cool-off of late summer or early autumn. Much of the highcountry requires long approaches on rocky trails through thick lodgepole pine and spruce forests, but its irresistible appeal draws hikers upward.

Subranges in the Southern Rockies include the red-tinted Sangre de Cristo of New Mexico and Colorado and the Sawatch and Elk Mountains of central Colorado. Farther north, the Front Range, Mummy Range, Never Summer Mountains, Flat Tops, and others profile the horizons. Unlike the more thoroughly glaciated western mountains or densely vegetated slopes of the Appalachians, highcountry in Colorado is often walkable on or off trail, with vast expanses of rolling terrain above timberline. Several roads reach above the trees, offering the opportunity to step directly out of the car and into Colorado highcountry veneered with lofty meadows that allow enthralling free-form wandering among ridges, saddles, and summits (but avoid trampling alpine wildflowers!). The downside in the Southern Rockies is that high elevation requires acclimatization for most visitors, and frequent afternoon thunderstorms with high exposure deserve extreme caution.

In Utah, the Uinta Mountains rise as the highest range aligned east-west outside Alaska. Their west end Ts into the north-south Wasatch Mountains, which boldly backdrop Salt Lake City and its suburban lineup sprawling for many miles.

Northward in Wyoming, monumental peaks and glaciers of the Wind River Range push skyward—a range with few rivals for its rugged exposure, wildness, and extreme gradient. North and west of there, and a poster child for the entire Rocky Mountain chain, the Tetons rank as the most dramatic uplift, with young peaks scraping the sky and sculpted to their craggy cores by glaciers. Northward and extending into Montana, notable ranges ring the Yellowstone Plateau, including, on its north side, the grizzly bear haunts of the Absaroka Mountains and, adjoining eastward, the hulking granite plateau of the Beartooths with their spacious U-shaped canyons. In central Idaho, the Sawtooth Mountains' escarpment reaches to ragged peaks yawning over a scenic valley floor, while other subranges of the Rockies adjoin to the east, north, and south.

In Montana, the spine of the Northern Rockies runs with scarcely a break to the Canadian border and beyond. Many aficionados regard the mountains of Glacier National Park as the most beautiful of the interior West. Geologically an extension of the Canadian Rockies, the park is famous for postcard views of vertical relief, Technicolor sedimentary strata, and evergreen forests. Glaciers nest in chilled northern enclaves, though their years are numbered in the age of global warming. Spectacular as any place, the Northern Rockies' elevations are lower than those farther south, and so acclimatization for hikers arriving from low elevations is not as difficult.

Much as the Black Hills are a distant outlier to the Rockies' east, the Blue Mountains lie to the west, across Hells Canyon of the Snake River, which marks the border of Idaho and Oregon. This 100-by-200-

mile expanse has seismically and volcanically risen from the far greater expanse of the Columbia Plateau, but the mostly forested slopes bear many similarities to the Rockies and so are included here.

The Rockies are well known for aspen-ringed meadows and rocky ridgelines that scribe almost any horizon across a huge swath of the West, but much of the region's acreage lies in forests, foothills, and valleys between the ranges. Most large valleys are now gridded with ranches, and their cottonwood riverfronts are diminished by diversions sucking water out of the mountain streams. Towns checker the larger valleys, and, at higher elevations, hardscrabble mining settlements have evolved into posh resorts for skiers and full-service recreation retreats in summer. These mountains also encompass some of the greatest expanses of wilderness in the Lower 48, with the largest blocks in the Yellowstone Ecosystem, central Idaho, and northwestern Montana.

Cathedral Spires, Black Hills

SOUTH DAKOTA

LOCATION: Custer State Park near Custer

LENGTH: 3 miles out and back, with longer hikes possible

ELEVATION: 6,584 feet at top; minor elevation gain

DIFFICULTY: easy to moderate

HIGHLIGHTS: pinnacles, ponderosa pine forest

The Black Hills are a low-elevation outlier of the Rockies 100 miles east of the main front and a topographic anomaly in the Great Plains. Better known for the chiseled presidential faces of Mount Rushmore, this range more naturally features the Cathedral Spires (or Needles).

Granite columns tower 200 feet above the forest—a hot spot for rock climbers since the 1930s. An otherwise easy trail requires a bit of scrambling and gets heavy use; arrive early or visit on weekdays or in spring and autumn.

From Highway 89 north of Custer, turn east on Highway 87 and drive 2.4 miles to the Cathedral Spires Trailhead (there is a state park fee). Other nearby trails climb 1,000 feet in 3.8 miles one way to the summit of Black Elk (formerly Harney) Peak in Black Hills National Forest, which, at 7,244 feet, is the highest mountain in the Dakotas. Park at Sylvan Lake near the intersection of Highways 87 and 89.

PREVIOUS SPREAD: Backlit by the sunrise, elk graze above timberline in Rocky Mountain National Park.

The Cathedral Spires form a ragged skyline in Black Hills National Forest south of Mount Rushmore.

La Luz Trail, Sandia Mountains

LOCATION: Cibola National Forest east of Albuquerque

LENGTH: 16 miles or less out and back, or 8 miles one way with a tram or road shuttle

ELEVATION: 10,678 feet at top of Sandia Peak; 7,040 feet at Juan Tabo Trailhead

DIFFICULTY: easy, then strenuous in the upper half

HIGHLIGHTS: rock walls, plant life ranging from desert to Rocky Mountains

Though isolated by desert terrain, the Sandia Mountains create a southern extension of the Rockies and rise abruptly at the northeastern doorstep of Albuquerque.

From the Juan Tabo Trailhead, hike the nicely designed La Luz Trail to Sandia Peak, with pinnacles, cliffs, and a biological tour from desert to Rocky Mountain forest—cacti to conifers in just a short walk. At the top, don't be disappointed by the crowd that opts to ride the tram from the east side of Albuquerque or to drive Route 536 to the crest from the other (east) side of the mountains.

Switchbacks in the lower half are terrific for trail runners. At 3 miles, the scenic benefits accrue wildly as the route enters pinyon pines, ponderosa pines, and Douglas firs among rock monoliths. At 4 miles, close-up views of pinnacles and sheer walls of the Sandia's upper slopes await.

Autumn is ideal, as ice may linger on the upper trail until May, and then it morphs quickly into a broiling summer. Take lots of water! Late in the day this trail earns its name—"the light"—as the desert sunset warms the remarkable scene. La Luz connects at the top with the North and South Crest Trails for longer Sandia tours.

From I-40 at the southeast side of Albuquerque, take exit 167 and then Tramway Boulevard/566 north for 9 miles to the Tramway turnoff. Continue 1 mile farther, turn right on Forest Road 333/Juan Tabo, and drive 2 miles uphill, bearing right to the Juan Tabo Trailhead and La Luz Trail. For an easier hike, some opt to use the tram one way. Ride up or down, using the 2.6-mile low-traverse connector trail that splits southward from La Luz 1 mile up from the bottom.

The La Luz Trail climbs to spectacular views at the base of the spires and cliffs of the Sandia Mountains at Albuquerque's urban edge.

OPPOSITE: From desert slopes with cholla cacti, yucca, and prickly pear, the La Luz Trail ascends the Sandia Mountains' escarpment and in only 3 miles enters the coniferous forests of the Rockies.

Wheeler Peak

LOCATION: northeast of Taos

LENGTH: 8 miles out and back

ELEVATION: 13,161 feet at top; 10,200 feet at trailhead

DIFFICULTY: moderate, but high elevation

HIGHLIGHTS: lake with a view, alpine slopes, highest peak in New Mexico

The Sangre de Cristo Range is the Rocky Mountains' southern uplift, running 250 miles from Salida, Colorado, to Santa Fe, New Mexico. Wheeler Peak is the high point of the southern end of this range and the towering summit of New Mexico. Don't confuse this Wheeler Peak with the one in Nevada.

The first mile follows an old road, followed by landlocked Williams Lake 2 miles out at 11,200 feet. About 200 yards before the lake, the summit trail turns left and switchbacks nicely for a 2,000-foot climb and a total out-and-back trip of 8 miles. Extended alpine wandering is possible on ridges rimming the immense cirque basin.

An easy gradient is complicated by elevation and weather; many hikers will want to acclimatize at high elevations beforehand. Check the forecast and avoid thunderstorms on this exposed approach that surmounts tree line at 11,000 feet, well below the summit. Watch for bighorn sheep. No permit to hike or camp is required, but consider weekdays and autumn to avoid crowds. June is the driest month for Wheeler, though consolidated snow may persist. New Mexico's July and August monsoon season brings threatening afternoon thunderstorms. September and early October are great. Even with a good weather forecast, launch this outing early in the day.

Some hikers opt for a longer hike from the Bull of the Woods Trailhead, starting lower near the upper end of the Taos Ski Valley area parking lot. This 16-mile round trip has long, exposed ridge-lines; be ready to bail downhill if storms approach.

From Taos, take Highway 522 north for 4 miles. Turn right on Highway 150, go 15 miles to the Taos Ski Valley area, bear left to the upper parking lot, and continue upward to the end of Twining Road for the Williams Lake Trailhead, to the right of the Bavarian Restaurant.

Scree slopes and high meadows of Wheeler Peak drop to forests of Douglas firs in the view east from the summit.

Black Face Mountain

Unlike linear ranges that typically stretch north-south without extended width, the San Juan Mountains of southern Colorado sprawl massively in an oval of acreage from Telluride to Pagosa Springs. The San Miguel Mountains subrange occupies the western end of this uplift, bounded on the southeast by Highway 145 at Lizard Head Pass. Here a trail up Black Face Mountain climbs with views of the 400-foot Lizard Head spire and Wilson Peak, Mount Wilson, and El Diente Peak—all topping 14,000 feet.

Drive south from Telluride on Highway 145 to Lizard Head Pass, park on the right, and take the trail northeast and then west to the summit of Black Face and its thrilling ridgeline path. Return, or for a loop 4 miles longer, continue southwest from Black Face and descend via Cross Mountain Trail, which nears Highway 145 farther south. Then return to the parking lot at the pass on a trail paralleling the highway.

Less accessible but nonetheless crowded, Chicago Basin and Columbine Pass is a popular backpacking trip at the heart of the San Juan Range. North of Durango, go to the Purgatory Creek Campground and Trailhead. Hike southeast to the Animas River, then up its canyon to Needle Creek at mile 9.6, then another 5 miles to Chicago Basin, and then steeply onward to Columbine Pass, with access to several 14,000-foot peaks. For an easier journey, make reservations and take the Durango and Silverton Narrow Gauge Railroad to Needleton—1 mile upstream from the confluence of Needle Creek and the Animas River—and walk from there.

LOCATION:	Lizard Head Pass south of Telluride
LENGTH:	7.6 miles out and back
ELEVATION:	12,147 feet at top; 10,250 feet at trailhead
DIFFICULTY:	strenuous, high elevation
HIGHLIGHTS:	views, easy access

From the ridgeline of Black Face Mountain, the Lizard Head spire aims skyward while Mount Wilson fills the background. Here the San Miguel subrange borders the greater San Juan Mountain complex of southern Colorado—one of the largest contiguous mountain masses in the West.

Independence Pass

LOCATION: White River National Forest east of Aspen

LENGTH: 1 to 10 miles out and back

ELEVATION: 13,198 feet at top; 12,095 feet at trailhead

DIFFICULTY: easy to moderate, but high elevation

HIGHLIGHTS: highcountry, immediate access

Independence is among the Rocky Mountains' most scenic passes, and it has road access for above-timberline hiking just out of your car. This is the highest paved road across the Continental Divide. Literally from the first step, hikers enter a world of alpine wonders.

From Aspen, drive east on Highway 82 for 19 miles. Park in the big Independence Pass lot and walk south on the busy path. Continue beyond the pavement and the crowd for 3 miles, ascending ridges to a 12,095-foot knob, and then up rocky scree to a 13,198-foot peak with views of Colorado's highest range—the north-south-aligned Sawatch—and also westward to the Williams Mountains above Aspen.

Back at the parking lot, paths north of the road also head to steep but walkable scree rising 2.5 miles with views eastward to Mount Elbert—at 14,443 feet the highest peak in Colorado and second highest in the United States outside Alaska. Climbing tops out on Twining Peak at 13,711 feet.

The parking lot at the pass fills, but turnover is high, as most people simply pause for short strolls. In early summer, high slopes offer excellent backcountry skiing, which sometimes lasts into July on northern aspects. Expect afternoon summer thunderstorms; hike early and descend from peaks and ridgelines before storms build. Independence Pass is snowbound and closed from November to late May.

A hiker explores user trails both south and north of Independence Pass with panoramas of Rocky Mountain peaks all around.

OPPOSITE: At Independence Pass, hikers can step directly out of their cars and into highcountry above timberline. In this view, spruce forests have been pruned into linear patterns between paths regularly pummeled by avalanches.

Maroon Bells-Snowmass Creek

COLORADO

LOCATION: southwest of Aspen

LENGTH: 2 miles out and back, 15 miles one way, or 26-mile loop

ELEVATION: 12,462 feet at top; 9,580 feet at Maroon Lake Trailhead

DIFFICULTY: easy to strenuous

HIGHLIGHTS: alpine lakes, aspen forests, views

Three peaks called Maroon Bells rank among the most-photographed mountains in America—a repeated image ever since scenic calendars first rolled off the press. At the end of the access road, appreciate the perfect composition—reflection and all—from the lake's outlet. Then tour the northern shore, rioting with wildflowers in midsummer. The trail climbs closer to the Bells' uplift and emerges in meadows at Crater Lake.

For the ultrafit, an exhilarating day hike or an easier-paced, two- to four-day backpack trip continues over Buckskin Pass at 12,462 feet, skirts the harsh beauty of Snowmass Lake, and, after the long descent of Snowmass Creek, emerges at Snowmass Creek Campground with road access and, if you have two cars, a shuttle road back to Aspen.

Beware that in summer cars are not allowed beyond a parking lot and shuttle-bus checkpoint on the Maroon Bells access road just south of Aspen (there is a fee). Transfer to the bus for drop-off at Maroon Lake. Expect crowds and a social atmosphere.

A more ambitious 26-mile loop circumnavigates the Bells clockwise, starting southeast of Maroon Lake via West Maroon, Frigid Air, Trail Rider, and Buckskin Passes, and then returning to Maroon Lake without the need for a shuttle. See the White River National Forest map.

Among the most-photographed Rocky Mountain scenes, the Maroon Bells reflect their signature warmth of color at sunrise.

Mount Massive

LOCATION: San Isabel National Forest southwest of Leadville

LENGTH: 13 miles out and back

ELEVATION: 14,421 feet at top; 10,000 feet at trailhead

DIFFICULTY: strenuous, high elevation

HIGHLIGHTS: summit of a Colorado 14er

Most of Colorado's 54 peaks of 14,000 feet and higher can be summited as walk-ups, and Mount Massive is one of the most accessible and amenable to fit and acclimatized hikers without advanced mountaineering skills. Yet, no slouch, it's Colorado's second-highest peak and the third-highest peak in the continental United States. Named well, it boasts the most acreage above 14,000 feet.

A boot-worn path is trod by many in summer. From the trailhead, walk north on the Colorado Trail and after 3 miles turn left onto the summit path. The rocky top can be reached with a long day hike, but only when afternoon thunderstorms do not threaten—rarely a reliable scenario. An option is to backpack several miles to timberline or nearby on the southeastern slope and then spring for the summit before daybreak in order to descend from high points by noon.

Take Highway 24 south from Leadville. At Route 300, turn west and continue 0.7 miles, then at Route 11 turn south and continue 1 mile. Turn right on gravel Halfmoon Road and continue 6.5 miles to the Mount Massive Trailhead just after crossing Halfmoon Creek (all closed by snow through May). This is also a trailhead to Colorado's highest summit, Mount Elbert, which also attracts a lot of hikers.

The route to Mount Massive departs from the Colorado Trail and entices hikers up the state's second-highest peak. Here the Sawatch Mountains of central Colorado crowd the horizon.

Loveland Pass

Loveland Pass lies within an hour's drive from Denver—assuming travelers avoid I-70's nightmare of weekend backups—and offers a rare opportunity to step into alpine terrain with nominal driving just a few miles off an interstate highway.

Start at a parking area barely north of the pass, cross the road, and follow user trails southwest and traverses wending westward across ridgelines. Or, on the other side of the road, go to the ridge of your choice and back.

To push the thin-air envelope here, hike east and south from the pass, where ridges connect to three 14ers—Grizzly, Torreys, and Grays—reaching out 6 miles from the pass. The spaciousness of high-country here makes quick escape difficult during thunderstorms, so watch the weather forecast. The high elevation of the pass and adjacent peaks will require acclimatization or may limit this alpine experience to a short walk, which alone is good.

On I-70 westbound from Denver, continue beyond Georgetown, take the Loveland Pass exit, and drive south and up to the pass.

LOCATION: south of I-70, west of Denver and Georgetown

LENGTH: 1 to 12 miles out and back

ELEVATION: 14,270 feet at top of Grays Peak; 11,992 feet at road access

DIFFICULTY: easy to strenuous, high elevation

HIGHLIGHTS: views above timberline, access to 14,000-foot peaks

Only a few miles from I-70, the Loveland Pass Highway delivers hikers directly onto spacious alpine terrain. Trails wander west from the pass and others trend east and south to 14,000-foot peaks.

Flattop Mountain

LOCATION: Rocky Mountain National Park

LENGTH: 8 miles out and back, with other options

ELEVATION: 12,363 feet at top of Ptarmigan Pass; 9,475 feet at eastern base at Bear Lake

DIFFICULTY: strenuous, high elevation

HIGHLIGHTS: Continental Divide, views

This popular trail gains nearly 3,000 feet to the Continental Divide and combines a long approach through pine and spruce forests with high meadows and miles of unobstructed views above timberline.

For a starting point that's closest to the Denver urban area, hike east to west. Park at the Bear Lake lot early in the morning or, better, take the shuttle bus from its base lower along Bear Lake Road—the only option after the parking lot fills (by 7:00 a.m.!). From the picturesque lake, hike north and then west on Flattop Mountain Trail. With nearly half the mileage crossing exposed highcountry, the route tops out at Ptarmigan Pass. Hallett Peak, immediately south of the pass, makes a rewarding add-on, where another 700 vertical feet of rock-stepping tops out at 12,713 feet.

This stellar long day hike returns to Bear Lake, but for an odyssey across the Continental Divide, take your loaded backpack and continue westward from the pass for another 10 miles downhill via campsites, forests, and meadows of Tonahutu Creek, ending at its trailhead at 8,720 feet on the northern side of Grand Lake. The gasoline for this interminable shuttle can be saved by hiking a multiday loop of 45 miles, returning eastward via the more southerly North Inlet Trail back to Flattop and Bear Lake. See Rocky Mountain National Park maps.

Day hiking here is unlimited, but permits for backpacking with assigned campsites in the park are required and in high demand; register with the Park Service online early in the year. Bear-proof canisters are also required.

To reach the eastern trailhead from Estes Park, take Highway 36 (Trail Ridge Road), but before climbing high go left on Bear Lake Road and continue to the bus station or road's end. For the western trailhead, take Highway 34 to Grand Lake,

The Flattop Mountain Trail crosses the Continental Divide in Rocky Mountain National Park, linking Bear Lake on the east side with Grand Lake at the western base of Colorado's Front Range.

turn east at Grand Lake Village on West Portal Road, and go 1 mile to the Tonahutu turnoff (left) and up to the trailhead.

Rocky Mountain National Park highlights the entire Middle and Southern Rockies and, while crowds thicken in summer, the attractions are magnetic—all the more amazing for lying so close to Denver's urban fringe. Trail Ridge Road ranks among America's finest drives above timberline; see elk, pikas, and marmots. With little effort there, stroll the Ute Trail across spacious alpine terrain.

The big fish in the park is Longs Peak—an extreme ascent for the ultrafit. From 9,405 feet, climb 8 steep miles one way to the summit at 14,259 feet (starting at 3:00 a.m. is recommended and a permit is required).

For the unacclimatized, minimize the high-elevation blues on streamfront trails in the southern end of the park, including the Wild Basin area via gravel road ending at the Ouzel and Thunder Lakes Trailheads. Even there parking lots fill, so arrive early to avoid using pulloffs down the dusty road.

OPPOSITE: In the highcountry of Rocky Mountain National Park, families of elk graze near Trail Ridge Road.

One of the quintessential mammals of high, rock-strewn mountainsides of the West, a furry pika harvests grass and forbs for winter storage (top). Ouzel Falls is a prime attraction along the Ouzel Lake Trail in the southern end of Rocky Mountain National Park (bottom).

Flat Tops Wilderness

LOCATION: White River and Routt National Forests south of Steamboat Springs

LENGTH: 11-mile loop

ELEVATION: 11,800 feet at top; 10,280 feet at trailhead

DIFFICULTY: moderate

HIGHLIGHTS: wildflowers, narrow ridgeline, views

This loop climbs through lush meadows with a full palate of wildflower colors in midsummer and crosses a thin outcrop traditionally known as Devil's Causeway (I call it "Heaven's Bridge")—a four-foot-wide bedrock dropping 80 feet on both sides and just barely connecting two high ridges.

Westward views open to Trappers Lake, where Forest Service landscape architect Arthur Carhart—confronted in 1919 with an assignment to develop cabin sites—instead initiated the agency's first recommendation for wilderness protection. Unusual among subranges of the Rockies, Flat Tops—no relation to Flattop Mountain—is a plateau of resistant rock with glacial basins, lakes, and stream valleys carved into its uplift.

The trail starts at the northern end of Stillwater Reservoir. Walk southwest 0.8 miles, and then turn right on Bear River Trail and climb 3 miles. Cross the Causeway, go another 1.2 miles, turn left on Chinese Wall Trail, and continue 2.4 miles. At Bear River Trail, turn left and continue 4 miles back to the parking lot.

From Steamboat Springs, drive south on Highway 40. At Highway 131, turn right, go south to Yampa, turn right on Moffat Avenue, and follow County Route 7 for 7 miles. Continue on gravel Forest Road 900 for 10 more miles to its end at Stillwater Reservoir and the trailhead.

The Devil's Causeway, or "Heaven's Bridge," in Flat Tops Wilderness decisively separates the White River basin to the west from the Yampa basin to the east.

OPPOSITE: South of Steamboat Springs, the Flat Tops Wilderness Trail climbs through meadows rioting in summer color.

Lake Blanche, Wasatch Mountains

LOCATION: Big Cottonwood Canyon southeast of Salt Lake City

LENGTH: 7 miles out and back, with longer options possible

ELEVATION: 8,920 feet at top; 6,200 feet at trailhead

DIFFICULTY: strenuous

HIGHLIGHTS: lake with mountain backdrop

Sundial Peak juts skyward here with its reflection in Lake Blanche—a classic hiking destination in the imposing Wasatch Range immediately east of Salt Lake City and its suburbs. While the more remote east side of the Wasatch has been sliced and diced by mining, this west side is principally wilderness. Blanche was once dammed, but the old rock structure has deteriorated. Just 5 miles from the urban area, expect crowds all summer, especially on weekends; hike early or on weekdays.

From I-15, go east on I-215, then at 190 turn east up Big Cottonwood Canyon and go 4.5 miles to the Mill B South Fork Trailhead. From the end of the parking lot, the rock-studded trail gains 2,726 feet. No permit is required for day or overnight use.

For more mountain exposure, continue beyond Lake Blanche to Lake Florence, where energetic hikers can continue east and south off trail for another 1.5 steep miles one way, and then with Class 3 scrambling climb Mount Superior at 11,132 feet. For this final pitch in early summer, carry an ice ax.

A quick ride from Salt Lake City, the Lake Blanche Trail climbs to the base of Sundial Peak.

Ostler Peak,
Uinta Mountains

LOCATION: Wasatch-Uinta-Cache National Forest south of Evanston

LENGTH: 13 miles out and back

ELEVATION: 10,800 feet at top; 8,800 feet at trailhead

DIFFICULTY: easy to moderate

HIGHLIGHTS: streams, lakes, Uinta peaks

Lying directly north of and adjoining the Wasatch Mountains, the Uinta Mountains are the largest among America's few east-west-aligned ranges outside Alaska. Unlike the jagged profile of some other Rocky Mountain subranges, many Uinta peaks appear like rounded domes at which glaciers have chewed northern exposures. Lofty perched plateaus narrow down to long, skinny ridgelines between summits. Streams have cut into the heart of the range and flow south or north.

This hike climbs easily through lush meadows. In 2 miles, stay left and ascend Ostler Fork of the Stillwater Fork of the Bear River. Undulant terrain rises to Ostler Lake—a worthy off-trail destination to the west, with good camping—while the trail continues to its end at the gem of Amethyst Lake, tucked into a glacial cirque shadowed by Ostler Peak and the impressive Uinta crest.

From Salt Lake City, take I-80 east to Silver Creek Junction and turn south on Highway 40. At 248, go east to Kamas and then continue onward on Route 150 (Mirror Lake Scenic Byway, closed in winter), which arcs east and then north. After starting the northbound descent toward Hayden Fork of the Bear River, turn right on Forest Road 057 and drive up Stillwater Fork of the Bear River to the Christmas Meadows Trailhead at the end.

Other Uinta Mountains trails beckon, including short hikes off the Mirror Lake Scenic Byway. Most extended Uinta routes require longer drives to remote points on the north side of the range farther east. Trails cross the uplift through five different passes.

After gradually gaining elevation along Stillwater and Ostler Forks of the Bear River, the Ostler Peak Trail leads to meadows and Amethyst Lake at the northern front of the Uinta Mountains—the nation's largest east-west-aligned range outside Alaska.

Vedauwoo Rocks

LOCATION: Medicine Bow National Forest east of Laramie

LENGTH: 3-mile loop

ELEVATION: 8,600 feet at top; 8,400 feet at lowest point

DIFFICULTY: easy

HIGHLIGHTS: boulder fields, granite cliffs, aspens, pines

The Rockies are not all lofty peaks. Small subranges rise as outliers and as lower terrain with easy access and longer seasons for hiking. The Medicine Bow Mountains, for example, are the first Rocky Mountain subrange that travelers encounter when heading west across I-80, and the Sherman Mountains are a smaller appendage just north of the interstate. Here the easily missed Vedauwoo (*VAY-da-voo*) Rocks tantalize as a prelude to large mountains and as a chance for adjusting to elevation.

The loop begins at Medicine Bow National Forest's West Turtle Rock Campground and encircles a mountain domed in granite boulders, passing through aspen and pine forests stunted by the spare terrain and emerging at the East Turtle Rock Trailhead, with a connecting path back to the start. Vedauwoo's vertical walls of textured granite attract rock climbers who can be seen on their athletic routes to the top.

On I-80 west of Cheyenne, take exit 329, drive northeast on Forest Road 720, and bear left to the West Turtle Rock Trailhead.

At the short hike circumnavigating Vedauwoo Rocks in Medicine Bow National Forest, domes of granite bulge behind thickets of ponderosa and lodgepole pines along with Engelmann spruces.

Titcomb Basin, Wind River Range

LOCATION: Bridger-Teton
National Forest east of Pinedale

LENGTH: 28 miles out and back

ELEVATION: 10,598 feet at
Titcomb Basin; 9,280 feet
at trailhead

DIFFICULTY: moderate but long

HIGHLIGHTS: granite
highcountry, alpine lakes,
glaciers

With no hyperbole, one can say that the Wind River Range is one of the most rugged mountain masses on the continent. For its length, width, and features—including cirques, moraines, arêtes, glaciers, granite walls, and cobalt-blue lakes perched high above timberline—the Winds have few rivals in America.

To reach the astonishing highcountry of this 100-mile-long lineup of peaks, several trailheads and enticing paths await, but this popular one starts northeast of Pinedale at Elkhart Park. The trail climbs through resinous forests to glaciated lakes and continues upward to the exquisitely barren, ice-scraped universe of Titcomb Basin. Lower connecting routes spin off to the north, south, and east, but the Titcomb Basin Trail abruptly dead-ends at the severity of the Wind River Range's ultimate barrier: sheer-wall granite. Off-trail hikers can explore perched lakes, snowy cirques, and the bases of peaks that soar vertically to the Continental Divide.

But just so you know: the Winds are insanely buggy from warm-up through midsummer or later. Repellant is a must. If you're going to use DEET once in your life, this is the place to do it. Also beware of thunderstorms. These problems dissipate in crisp autumn with exquisite days but cold nights; watch for early snowfall.

From Pinedale, drive northeast on Forest Road 134 past Fremont Lake for 16 miles to the road's end at the Elkhart Park Trailhead.

Another Wind River attraction with an irresistible name, Cirque of the Towers, lies southward in the range with access via Big Sandy Campground, 24 miles south of Pinedale.

Coniferous forests thicken the west slope of the Wind River Range near the trailhead to Titcomb Basin.

OPPOSITE: The Wind River Range of south-central Wyoming is one of the most rugged, glaciated, and vertical topographies in the West—a highlight of austere mountain wildness.

Cascade-Paintbrush Loop

LOCATION: Grand Teton National Park

LENGTH: 25-mile loop, with longer hikes possible

ELEVATION: 9,035 feet at Lake Solitude; 6,783 feet at trailhead

DIFFICULTY: moderate to strenuous

HIGHLIGHTS: Teton views, cascading streams

Grand Teton National Park houses the most iconic mountain images in America. From the valley floor, peaks rise 7,000 feet to glacier-carved but resistant summits of South, Middle, and Grand Teton (the second-highest mountain in Wyoming), plus other photogenic landmarks, such as Teewinot, Owens, and Moran. The fault block that forms the precipitous eastern face of the range is among the most dramatic in the United States.

Ultraclassic, the Cascade-Paintbrush Loop tours canyons and circumnavigates jaw-dropping peaks immediately north of the highest mountain group. Hike either way: up Cascade to its forks and then jog north to return down Paintbrush, or vice versa. A base-level trail connects the two canyon routes along the west shore of Jenny Lake. The loop makes a splendid two-day or longer backpacking trip with compelling opportunities for day hiking to additional highcountry at the heart of the Teton Range.

A thrilling 10-mile out-and-back digression from upper elevations of this hike nears the west face of Grand Teton and leads to Schoolroom Glacier at 10,338 feet. Other adjoining trails connect with an intricate backpacking network throughout the Teton Range.

Those who are game for a longer loop can ascend Paintbrush to the top at Lake Solitude, turn south and continue past the highest peaks to Alaska Basin, and then descend Death Canyon to a car shuttle for 34 miles of hiking—or walk back north from Death Canyon on lowcountry connectors to Jenny Lake for 45 miles total. And another Teton epic continues from highcountry southward across the perched Death Canyon Shelf to Marion Lake and down to a parking lot south of Phelps Lake for a car shuttle.

The Teton Range caps Grand Teton National Park, and the high peaks' backdrop to the Snake River endures as one of the most iconic scenic views of the American West.

Beware of thunderstorms, steep surprises in snowfield glissading, and early season bugs. Grizzly bears have also returned to the Tetons; take precautions. Backpacking permits are required from the National Park Service, with strict quotas on numbers for these popular hikes; apply early and be ready to share the mountains.

Take Highway 26 north from Jackson to Moose, turn left on Teton Park Road, and go to a trailhead on the southeast side of Jenny Lake or a bit farther to the east side of String Lake.

The northwestern face of Grand Teton overshadows upper Cascade Canyon (top). Headwaters of Cottonwood Creek near the base of the Cascade-Paintbrush Loop foam through a lodgepole pine forest recovering from past fires. High peaks of the Teton Range rise in the background (bottom).

OPPOSITE: Seen from a short side trip off the Cascade-Paintbrush Loop, Grand Teton's vertical northwestern face veers skyward above the South Fork of Cascade Creek.

Middle Teton

LOCATION: Grand Teton National Park

LENGTH: 13 miles out and back

ELEVATION: 12,804 feet at top; 6,732 feet at trailhead

DIFFICULTY: extreme

HIGHLIGHTS: rushing streams, major summit, view to Grand Teton

The Teton Range's jagged summits challenge experienced climbers and offer some of the most renowned ascents in America. Grand Teton requires advanced skills and roped belay, but Middle Teton, after early summer's melt-off, can be summited by hikers who are competent with potentially treacherous snowbanks and a bouldered couloir ascending to the top of this peak and its breathtaking vantage.

From the Lupine Meadows Trailhead north of Moose, hike 4 miles up Garnet Canyon to the main trail's end at the climbers' campground. The next morning, strike out on paths to the southwest side of Middle Teton, then climb its couloir with rocky scrambling. Take care to avoid the steepest parts of the snowfields, especially when returning and descending convex slopes that can curve into uncontrollable pitches. A tempting glissade can easily accelerate to an uncontrolled slide ending in sharp granite (I know).

Campsite permits are required by the National Park Service and are limited. Mid- to late summer is best for this challenging hike and climb. Take Highway 26 north from Jackson, turn west at Moose, and continue to the Lupine Meadows Trailhead.

Beyond the Garnet Canyon backcountry camping area, the rock-strewn route to Middle Teton's summit steps upward over glacial moraines and onto snowfields, bedrock, and jagged ridgelines framing the southern face of the mountain.

OPPOSITE: A rigorous scramble to the top of Middle Teton opens views to severe rockscapes of the western Teton Range.

Gros Ventre Mountains

WYOMING

This Gros Ventre Loop visits stunning mountains that see far less use than the nearby Teton Range, and it penetrates country of entirely different geologic makeup, with high plateaus, broad summits, and layered sedimentary rock.

From the trailhead upstream from Granite Creek Falls, cross to the east side of the stream, walk south (downstream) 1.5 miles, and turn east (uphill) on the Swift Creek Trail. Cross the Granite Creek-Crystal Creek divide, pass the incline of Black Peak (consider its seductive off-trail excursion), and continue north down Crystal Creek. After 6 miles, turn west toward Burnt Point on the West Fork Crystal Creek Trail and climb 6 miles to an enchanting plateau with off-trail destinations, including Pyramid Peak to the south. Descend into the upper Flat Creek basin and turn left (south) on Trail 3014, dropping to the Granite Creek headwaters and a 6-mile descent back to the trailhead. Take the Bridger-Teton National Forest map.

From Jackson, go south on Highway 89. At Hoback Junction, turn east on Route 191 and drive 12 miles up the Hoback River to the gravel Granite Creek Road. Turn left and continue to the trailhead at the end.

> **LOCATION:** Bridger-Teton National Forest east of Jackson
>
> **LENGTH:** 30-mile loop
>
> **ELEVATION:** 10,660 feet at top; 6,987 feet at trailhead
>
> **DIFFICULTY:** moderate to strenuous and long
>
> **HIGHLIGHTS:** streams, wildflower meadows, mountain ridges and walls

Backcountry skiers approach the divide between Swift and Crystal Creeks in the Gros Ventre Wilderness.

Beartooth Pass

LOCATION: southwest of Red Lodge, Montana

LENGTH: 0.5- to 2-mile loop

ELEVATION: 10,947 feet at top; some options drop 500 feet

DIFFICULTY: easy to moderate

HIGHLIGHTS: high glaciated granite and meadows, views into deep canyons, easy access

The Beartooth Mountains are one of the West's most impressive road-accessible granitic formations soaring boldly and emphatically above timberline. This remarkable range lies just northeast of Yellowstone National Park and immediately east of the spaciously wild Absaroka Range.

The Beartooths are a unique granitic pluton that has been uplifted—not so much as peaks but rather a massive and bulky highcountry plateau—and now dissected into U-shaped canyons 4,000 feet deep. Fully in view from pullouts along the road, these are thrilling sights to behold. The dropoffs ultimately descend southward to Wyoming's upper Clarks Fork of the Yellowstone River or northward to Rock Creek, Montana.

Walkers can embark from multiple pullouts on the Beartooth Highway, stroll undulant ground, and then carefully flirt with steeper topography that accelerates downward thousands of feet. From the large summit parking lot, explore west or cross the road to the southeast side and follow ridgelines eastward down to breathtaking views of Gardner and Black Stone Lakes in glacial cirques. Watch for mountain goats; I've always found them here. But lay low and observe from a distance.

From Red Lodge, Montana, take Highway 212 southwest and up the paved switchbacks (open only in summer) to sky-splitting heights of the plateau. Or, from the northeastern corner of Yellowstone, drive to Cooke City, Montana, and then northeast on Highway 212 toward Red Lodge.

Incomparable views await within short strolls from the Beartooth Highway as it crests the massive granite plateau between Cooke City and Red Lodge, Montana.

Lake Fork and West Fork Rock Creek

MONTANA

LOCATION: Custer National Forest southwest of Red Lodge

LENGTH: 1 to 20 miles out and back, or 21 miles point to point

ELEVATION: 11,045 feet at Sundance Pass; 7,202 feet at Lake Fork Trailhead

DIFFICULTY: easy, short hikes, strenuous loop

HIGHLIGHTS: mountain streams, moose, high peaks

Beneath the awesome highcountry of Beartooth Pass, and to the north, forks of Rock Creek tumble through canyons carved by glaciers. My favorite— the trail up Lake Fork—shows off the rushing freshet with forests interspersed by avalanche chutes and thickets of willows and alders, making excellent habitat for moose, often seen browsing and supervising their calves along the trail's lower reaches.

For a day hike of 1 to 20 miles up Lake Fork and back, take Highway 212 southwest from Red Lodge for 9 miles, turn right on Lake Fork Road, and proceed 2 miles to the end.

Hiking up West Fork Rock Creek is a bit less scenic; slopes there burned in 2008. Drive just south of Red Lodge, turn right on West Fork Road, and go 10 miles to the end.

A three-day backpack trip can be taken up either of these forks, over Sundance Pass, and down the other fork for a 21-mile total (with a car shuttle). Be aware of bears, as this is grizzly country.

An easy walk up the Lake Fork Trail follows the rushing stream with views to crags of the Beartooth Plateau.

Moose frequent riparian thickets along the Lake Fork Trail.

OPPOSITE: On the West Fork Rock Creek Trail, hiker Bob Banks passes through areas burned by recent forest fires. The trail climbs to Sundance Pass and connects to the adjacent Lake Fork Trail.

Pettit-Toxaway Loop

LOCATION: Sawtooth National Recreation Area north of Ketchum

LENGTH: 18-mile loop

ELEVATION: 9,390 feet at top; 7,000 feet at trailhead

DIFFICULTY: moderate to strenuous

HIGHLIGHTS: mountain lakes, high pass, granite peaks

Within the Rockies, the Sawtooth Mountains come the closest to matching the exemplary grandeur of the Teton Range. Extending 40 miles north-south, this breathtaking uplift rises from sagebrush of the upper Salmon River basin to jagged ridgelines topping 10,000 feet. Glacial lakes lap bedrock shores while crystalline streams careen down the eastern face of the range and also off the ramped west slant to the Boise River. Renowned for superb trails—350 miles worth—the Sawtooths' routes traverse slopes with windswept conifers and cross granite platforms perched above timberline.

This loop begins at Pettit Lake, climbs to the jewel of Alice Lake, ascends 2,000 feet more to Toxaway Divide, then loops back eastward via Farley Lake and a short cutoff trail returning to the Pettit Lake Trailhead. A rigorous day hike here is better as an overnight with opportunities to wander the towering ridgelines, including a 1-mile scramble to Snowyside Peak at 10,651 feet.

From Ketchum, take Highway 75 to Sawtooth Valley. At 2 miles past the Alturas Lake intersection, turn left and continue to Pettit Lake's north shore and the Tin Cup Trailhead.

The Pettit-Toxaway Loop sees a lot of use. For a lonelier, longer, more epic Sawtooth expedition of 28 miles, enter farther north at Hell Roaring Lake; hike past Imogene, Edith, and Virginia Lakes; angle north past The Temple to Upper Cramer Lake; and descend via Redfish Lake to a car shuttle at the busy Redfish outlet area.

With similar rewards, the high-perched Sawtooth Lake, ensconced in rock and encircled by Sawtooth peaks, can be reached with a rigorous hike from the Iron Creek Trailhead west of Stanley.

An excellent Sawtooth Mountains backpacking trip climbs to Hell Roaring Lake and the Finger of Fate, and then continues northward and exits at Redfish Lake.

OPPOSITE: The Pettit-Toxaway Loop leads to crystal-clear lakes and a high pass in the Sawtooth Mountains.

Bench Lakes and Mount Heyburn

IDAHO

LOCATION: Sawtooth National Recreation Area south of Stanley

LENGTH: 10 miles out and back

ELEVATION: 8,200 feet at top; 6,560 feet at trailhead

DIFFICULTY: strenuous, with mountaineering options beyond

HIGHLIGHTS: scenic lake, craggy mountain views, access to high peaks

From the magnetic setting of Redfish Lake—as pretty as the road-accessible Rockies get—take the Bench Lakes Trail from the north side of Redfish and hike southward, traversing above the lake's west shore. Bear right in 2.5 miles to First, Second, and the smaller Third Bench Lakes, all buggy affairs where many hikers stop but fail to get the best views. Follow unlikely user paths uphill to a large lake nestled against bare rock tilting toward looming crags of Mount Heyburn.

After lingering snowpacks of early summer have melted (including dicey snow slopes angling into the lake described above), hikers who are game can continue climbing steeply southwest to the fifth and uppermost Bench Lake, eminently rock clad at 8,623 feet. Mount Heyburn towers like a geographic deity to its left, with a ridge that's walkable until the abrupt escarpment and climbers' domain begins. Go in late summer to minimize snow and billions of bugs.

From Ketchum, take Highway 75 toward Stanley, but 4 miles short of it turn southwest toward Redfish Lake. Half a mile back from the shoreline, park at the Fishhook Creek Trailhead.

Fourth Bench Lake reflects the craggy Mount Heyburn near the northern end of Idaho's magnificent Sawtooth Range.

Bitterroot Mountains

LOCATION: Montana-Idaho border south of Missoula

LENGTH: 6 miles out and back

ELEVATION: 9,000 feet at top; 6,100 feet at trailhead

DIFFICULTY: very strenuous

HIGHLIGHTS: views to the Bitterroots

The Bitterroots' 130-mile length constitutes the rugged border of Idaho and Montana and forms the heart of the 1.3-million-acre Selway-Bitterroot Wilderness—the fourth-largest wilderness complex in 49 states (or the largest when combined with the adjacent River of No Return in Idaho).

Access to the range is typified by long woodland trails that ascend canyons draining eastward to Montana's Bitterroot River Valley. Miles of hiking up these pure rushing streams is eventually rewarded with spacious highcountry of lichen-darkened granite, but a more abrupt ascent awaits north of Stevensville, Montana. From Bass Creek Campground, drive the dirt road for 7 steep miles to its end, where you might think you should be topping out, but, in fact, the trip has just begun.

Just beyond the parking area, appreciate the immediate view southward to a lineup of pinnacled crags—one of the more dramatic features of the Bitterroot chain. For the hike, trek uphill to the west. A buggy, wooded ridge route soon offers another thrilling view, and then the path veers relentlessly upward. Favor the ridgeline when you hear an otherwise tempting stream to the north, and when the path fades in definition, continue up to scree and snowfields with views to canyon voids and the Bass Creek crags at the raw heart of the Bitterroots. Grizzlies live here, so take precautions.

From Stevensville, drive on Highway 93 north 4 miles. Turn west on Bass Creek Road, go 3 miles to the creek's campground and lower trailhead, and then bend north on the dirt road (Forest Road 1136) and persist to the end.

For an easier hike, park down at the Bass Creek Campground Trailhead and walk upstream. Or choose the Blodgett Creek hike, secluded west of Hamilton, Montana, for its vertical walls and streamside ramp to Bitterroot heights.

A rugged trail climbs 3,000 feet from the road-end overlook north of Bass Creek Canyon, emerging with views to dramatic crags of the Bitterroot Range.

OPPOSITE: Northwest of Stevensville, Montana, Bass Creek Road winds up the front of the Bitterroot Mountains to a trailhead and view to the south.

Highline Trail

MONTANA

LOCATION: Glacier National Park

LENGTH: 1 to 15 miles out and back, with longer backpacking options

ELEVATION: 7,024 feet at Haystack Pass; 6,646 feet at trailhead

DIFFICULTY: easy but potentially long

HIGHLIGHTS: mountain views, wildlife

When it comes to mountain trails, Highline is the American masterpiece. For a casual or vigorous day hike, or an extended backpack trip connecting to other destinations, this Glacier National Park route is incomparable. It's a direct way to inhale the flavor of the Northern Rockies and one of the finest step-out-of-the-car highcountry trails in the West. It has the best easily accessed panoramas that resemble classic alpine scenery of the European Alps, which, for many, describe a standard of mountain beauty.

Unique to the United States, the Northern Rockies near the Canadian border are vividly colored, horizontal metamorphic and sedimentary strata stacked up like crystallized psychedelic cake layers. Stripes of red, maroon, gray, and black showcase complex geologic phenomena while glacial erosion has been extreme, all yielding distinctive terrain with spacious canyons and valleys. Conifers darken lesser slopes and cottonwoods green the cascading streamfronts at lower levels. Altogether the effect is thrilling in its depth and exceedingly grand openness, which are both found in the great U-shaped glaciated canyons of the West. These views welcome hikers every step of the way along Highline as it clings to cliffs, fords ice-water freshets, and wends through wildflower meadows.

The Garden Wall section begins only a half mile from the big Logan Pass parking lot. The trail's narrow shelf has been chiseled into the cliff with vertical walls above and below. A cable handrail adds security and, though easy, this path's exposure is not for the acutely acrophobic. The park's highcountry here and elsewhere offers views to lingering glaciers that are rapidly disappearing in the age of global warming.

Beyond the immediate scenic extravaganza, wildlife sightings are a bonus: bighorn sheep often

The Highline Trail exits the parking lot at Logan Pass and immediately enters stunning terrain of the Northern Rockies with its chiseled passage across the Garden Wall.

appear at close range, mountain goats wander into view, and ground squirrels and marmots whistle and scurry at your feet (do not feed them!). Grizzly bears are occasionally seen in the meadows and on the trail. Just so you're not disappointed, know that rangers occasionally close the trail because of bear activity—a rule you definitely want to follow. Always avoid brushy areas with poor visibility off trail, and make noise when approaching blind bends.

Even a short Highline walk is special. But in 6.8 miles, a spur trail turns right for a half mile up to the memorable Grinnell Glacier Overlook. After another mile on Highline, and just before the Glacier Park Chalet, another right turn leads in 1 mile to the Continental Divide at the broad saddle of Swiftcurrent Pass. Continue a half mile beyond for views of the east-wall free fall and its glaciers. Back at the chalet (which offers lodging, but it is in high demand and requires reservations), many hikers continue north on Highline and drop 4 miles to the west-side loop of Going-to-the-Sun Road, where they catch the shuttle bus back to Logan Pass. I prefer walking the return route to Logan in order to eyeball this remarkable landscape from both directions, and I always see wonders I missed on the way in.

For a backpacking adventure, Highline connects to trails northwestward, and also eastward over Swiftcurrent Pass and its subsequent free fall of switchbacks.

A key attraction in this extremely popular national park, Highline sees heavy use, but that's not necessarily a bad thing for casual travelers in

A bighorn sheep grazes along the Highline Trail (top). At an early age, mountain goats in Glacier National Park grow accustomed to hikers (bottom).

OPPOSITE: The Highline Trail edges the Continental Divide as hikers easily traverse highcountry in Glacier National Park.

grizzly country. Early morning and late afternoon are less-social times to enjoy this amazing place, as is autumn.

The entire national park offers 700 miles of trails. Once beyond the arterials, hikers leave crowds behind. The Park Service requires back-packing permits. Take all precautions, including food canisters, for grizzly bears here, as disturbing attacks have occurred in the past. In remote back-country, travel in a group of two or ideally more.

From Glacier National Park's west or east entrances, take Going-to-the-Sun Road up the winding highway to Logan Pass and walk north from the parking lot. Ride the tour bus to avoid congestion and parking snarls at peak hours, which start as early as 8:00 a.m.

The masterpiece of mountain trails, Highline offers a 17-mile round-trip day hike from Going-to-the-Sun Road at Logan Pass to Swiftcurrent Pass.

Grinnell Glacier

LOCATION: Glacier National Park

LENGTH: 11 miles out and back

ELEVATION: 8,355 feet at Grinnell Glacier; 6,515 feet at trailhead

DIFFICULTY: moderate, but a long day hike

HIGHLIGHTS: views, remnant glaciers, glacial lake and cirque, wildlife

From the Many Glacier area at the northeast side of Glacier National Park, this trail begins along the west shore of Swiftcurrent Lake, continues above Lake Josephine, ascends a forested valley, emerges in high meadows and fell-fields, and ends at the ice-sculpted outflow of Grinnell Glacier, with its icebergs, waterfalls at both inflow and outflow, and vertical-wall cirque backed by forbidding peaks.

At the end of the trail, hikers can stroll the lakeshore to the ice's edge (this is true as of this writing, though the ice is receding). Grinnell is the largest glacier in Glacier National Park and has been the second largest in the Rockies south of Canada—an opportunity to see a remnant glacier without rigorous climbing. (Emmons Glacier, on Mount Rainier in Washington, is the largest in 49 states.) In 1850, 150 glaciers were counted in the national park; by 2015 there were only 25. Glaciologists estimate that all will disappear by 2030, and global warming predictions have almost universally been underestimated.

From Highway 89, on the east side of the park, drive north to the Many Glacier/Lake Sherburne turnoff, go west to Swiftcurrent Lake's dock and trailhead, and walk west and south.

The Grinnell Glacier Trail reaches its climax at an ice-edged lake fed by the rapidly receding glacier.

FOLLOWING SPREAD: As remnants of the Rockies' greatest glacier south of Canada, icebergs float in the cirque-basin lake at the end of this spectacular hike to the heart of Glacier National Park (left). With its headwall at the Continental Divide, Grinnell Glacier melts into waterfalls (right).

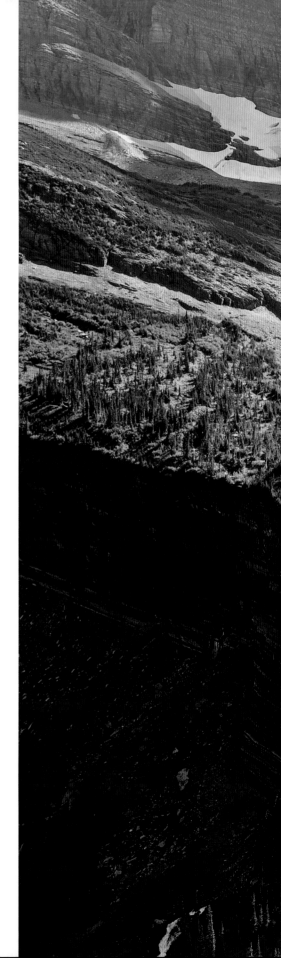

Piegan Pass

LOCATION: Glacier National Park

LENGTH: 10 miles out and back, or 14 miles via Siyeh Pass

ELEVATION: 7,600 feet at top; 5,800 feet at Siyeh Bend Trailhead

DIFFICULTY: moderate

HIGHLIGHTS: cascading streams, highcountry traverse, views to glaciers

Starting at Siyeh Bend on Going-to-the-Sun Road in Glacier National Park, the Piegan Pass Trail traverses to a high divide.

OPPOSITE: Mottled by cupped patterns of melting overhead, a snow cave has been hollowed by runoff under a deep drift near Piegan Pass.

With access directly off Going-to-the-Sun Road 2.2 miles east of Logan Pass, this hike climbs 3.8 miles to meadows at Preston Park (beware of bears here). Continue to the left for 2 more miles to Piegan Pass and roam this high platform for its fabulous views northward (get a map at the national park visitor center). A fascinating ice cave awaited there on my last trip.

Return to Preston Park and, for a longer outing of 14 miles total, go left (east) on the Siyeh Pass Trail and climb to breathtaking views eastward down Boulder Creek. Continue southeast and downward in the Baring Creek drainage leading to Sunrift Gorge and back to Going-to-the-Sun Road, now 3 miles east of the trip's start. Catch a free park shuttle bus from July through September, or hitch up the road to the trip's origin.

Eagle Cap, Wallowa Mountains

OREGON

LOCATION: Wallowa-Whitman National Forest south of Enterprise

LENGTH: 16-mile loop

ELEVATION: 8,560 feet at top; 5,591 feet at trailhead

DIFFICULTY: moderate

HIGHLIGHTS: scenic streamfront, lakes, granite peaks

Though the Wallowa Mountains of northeastern Oregon are a distinctive range lying west of the Rockies, they are included here for their similarities and closeness to the Rocky Mountain chain.

For this Wallowa Mountain hike, start at the Two Pan Trailhead near the confluence of the Lostine and East Lostine Rivers and walk south up the East Lostine into the heart of the Wallowa Range. After 7 miles, campsites appear at Mirror Lake and nearby. From Upper Lakes, which lie east of Mirror Lake, the 9,595-foot summit of Eagle Cap can be added to this hike on snowfields that prevail through midsummer. Go after July to minimize bugs.

For the looped return, go west from Mirror Lake 3.4 miles across a scenic divide toward the main-stem Lostine River, turn north near Minam Lake, and descend 6 miles down the Lostine and back to the trailhead.

To reach the Two Pan Trailhead, take Highway 129 south of Clarkston, Washington (which becomes Highway 3 in Oregon) to Highway 82, turn right and continue to Lostine, and then turn left (south) on the washboarded Lostine River Road. Or, from La Grande, Oregon, take Highway 82 north and east to Lostine and up. Get a permit, with no limits on numbers, at the trailhead.

Another hiking loop lies to the east. From a trailhead south of Joseph and nearby Wallowa Lake, trek up the West Fork Wallowa River to Frazier Lake and circle clockwise through a chain of lakes, returning to the West Fork for a rigorous circuit of 21 miles. However, this route gets extremely heavy and dusty horse traffic.

In Oregon's northeastern corner, the Wallowa Mountains showcase granite summits, glaciated peaks, and evergreen slopes. Here Eagle Cap rises over lakes at its base, and its runoff nourishes a radial pattern of rivers fanning out from this isolated range.

The Wallowa Mountains offer 540 miles of trails in all. Beyond that, the greater Blue Mountain complex across the northeastern quadrant of Oregon includes riverfront paths along the North Fork John Day, Malheur, and North Fork Malheur Rivers, as well as little-traveled routes into higher country of the Strawberry and Elkhorn Mountain subranges.

Perched in the divide between the Wallowa and Lostine Rivers, Mirror Lake reflects its surrounding walls, snowfields, and forests of pine and fir.

DESERT AND DRYLAND RANGES

Often overlooked as mountain ranges because aridity can overwhelm the senses here, drylands of the West span from the Rockies to the Sierra Nevada and from the steppes of eastern Oregon southward to Mexico. Major regions include the Great Basin Province of high ridges separating landlocked valleys mostly in Nevada (also called Basin and Range); the Colorado Plateau of arresting red-rock canyons in western Colorado, southern Utah, and northern Arizona; and southwestern "sky islands"—isolated ranges separated by harsh desert flats in Arizona and New Mexico.

These mountains are the driest in America—some a moonscape of volcanic rock rubble, especially barren in the blistering hot south—yet they also host strongholds of life. The Spring Mountains lurch skyward just west of Las Vegas with unexpected slopes whitened in winter and greened by bristlecone pines thousands of years old. These and other ranges receive enough snow at their highest elevations for an artistic mix of meadows, aspens, and conifers above ubiquitous sagebrush. Though the desert regions have some of the least-populated mountains, much of the backcountry has been heavily bladed by mining roads, and ranchers graze cattle wherever a trickle of water can be found or pumped from underground.

Unlike higher and more northerly ranges, southern mountains here offer great hiking in winter. Spring is delightfully fresh with snowmelt from the high peaks and the greening of desert plants. Summer sears, but in the more southerly regions it greens again after July's monsoons. Autumn cools with warm days and crisp nights. When off trail in the desert—and especially in the Colorado Plateau and southern areas—do not walk on the fragile dark crust of the biologically rich cryptogamic soil. Instead, carefully favor stone-stepping, eroded washes, and bedrock, even when it means detours.

Wheeler Peak

LOCATION: Great Basin National Park east of Ely

LENGTH: 10 miles out and back

ELEVATION: 13,063 feet at top; 10,160 feet at trailhead

DIFFICULTY: strenuous, high elevation

HIGHLIGHTS: summit climb, expansive Great Basin views, bristlecone pines

Wheeler is Nevada's second-highest peak (the 13,143-foot Boundary Peak in the White Mountains is shared with California) and rises 7,500 feet above sagebrush flats and playas at the center of the Great Basin Desert (another Wheeler Peak caps the mountains of New Mexico).

With Wheeler as the high point, the Snake Mountains align—like 50 other ranges across Nevada—on a north-south axis where rifting, or spreading of the continental plate, has resulted in ridgelines isolated by landlocked valleys. Above the sage and rabbitbrush, aspens grow as they do in the Rockies, along with eight species of conifers, some sculpted into dwarf krummholz at high elevations.

From the trailhead near the end of Wheeler Peak Road, the summit route ramps up the west side. The only permanent ice field in the Great Basin is still found as a remnant here on the north slope. Prepare for cold and thin air at Wheeler's windy heights, which require acclimatization by most hikers arriving from low elevations.

A separate and less rigorous trail beginning at the upper campground climbs 2 miles to a mountainside of charismatic bristlecone pines. Sculpted by wind, these trees live longer than any others in the world—some nearly 5,000 years and looking the part. The trail continues another 600 vertical feet to a "rock glacier" persisting where ice from an earlier and cooler climatic era remains buried under rockfall and moraine deposits at the base of Wheeler's soaring 2,000-foot headwall.

From Highway 50 in eastern Nevada, take 487 south, turn west on 488, enter Great Basin National Park, and ascend its paved road to campgrounds and trailheads.

PREVIOUS SPREAD: The view from Ajo Peak in Organ Pipe Cactus National Monument stretches out to isolated sky islands of the southwestern desert in Arizona.

At 13,063 feet, Wheeler Peak ranks among the tallest in the desert regions and fills the background from the end of the Bristlecone Pine and Rock Glacier Trails in Great Basin National Park.

Spring Mountains

LOCATION: Humboldt-Toiyabe National Forest west of Las Vegas

LENGTH: 1 to 6 miles out and back

ELEVATION: 9,380 feet at top; 8,470 feet at trailhead

DIFFICULTY: easy to moderate

HIGHLIGHTS: bristlecone pines, views to the Nevada desert

Few expect ancient pines to rise on an astonishing landscape within sight of Las Vegas, but they do on high slopes of the Spring Mountains. From the Bristlecone Trailhead, a gravel path loops through a remarkable grove of weathered Methuselahs, some dead but still standing for 2,000 years! This bristlecone grove of 18,000 acres is among the largest in the West.

Day hikers can continue up ridgelines to higher ground on Mount Charleston at 11,918 feet—often snowbound through April. Be careful here in off-trail travel; don't inadvertently wander into vaguely defined and homogeneous adjacent drainages and return toward an unexpected location below, as I once did on heavy springtime snow cover.

From Las Vegas, take Highway 95 north, continue past Route 157 (Kyle Canyon Road), and go west on Route 156 (Lee Canyon Road). Enter the Spring Mountains National Recreation Area, pass the McWilliams and Dolomite Campground turn-offs, and park at the Bristlecone Trailhead.

A startling surprise within the Great Basin's width across Nevada, the Spring Mountains create the western skyline seen from Las Vegas and catch enough snowfall to support a remarkable array of ancient bristlecone pines.

Ramparts Trail, Cedar Breaks

LOCATION: Cedar Breaks National Monument east of Cedar City

LENGTH: 4 miles out and back

ELEVATION: 10,350 feet at trailhead, with a 600-foot drop

DIFFICULTY: easy, but high elevation

HIGHLIGHTS: rock formations, bristlecone pines

Mountains of the southwestern desert take many forms, and the Cedar Breaks uplift of golden cliffs is exceptional. The geography that delivers spectacular canyons in Zion National Park and pinnacles in Bryce Canyon ramps continuously up to the mountain bastion of Cedar Breaks—the youngest layer of the "Grand Staircase" of Colorado Plateau sedimentary rocks. Here the ancient river-delta sandstone has been sheared off and exposed by the Hurricane Fault, where the plateau meets the Great Basin Province to the west. Rocks luminously colored orange, yellow, white, and red confront forests of limber pines, Engelmann spruces, and bristlecone pines—together a striking landscape of green and gold under violet skies.

Designated in 1933 by President Franklin Roosevelt, this national monument enjoys protection comparable to that of a national park. Similarly safeguarded, other desert monuments at Grand Staircase-Escalante and Bears Ears have recently been subject to attempted reductions in size to allow gas and oil development.

For easy walking at Cedar Breaks, take the popular Ramparts Trail downhill from the visitor

At Spectra Point in Cedar Breaks National Monument, bristlecone pines have endured for thousands of years.

OPPOSITE: At Cedar Breaks National Monument, seismic faulting has exposed multiple layers of sandstone and other sedimentary rock formations capping the Colorado Plateau.

center, though be prepared on the return for thin air at 10,000 feet. About halfway down, at Spectra Point, sculptural bristlecone pines appear with marmots scurrying between dens. This hike is prime at sunset's golden glow. Higher and cooler than Zion and Bryce Canyon National Parks, Cedar Breaks allows for escaping the bustle of those popular desert attractions.

From I-15 at Cedar City, drive east on Highway 14, and then turn north on 148. After entering the national monument, go left to the visitor center and trailhead.

San Francisco Peaks

LOCATION: Coconino National Forest north of Flagstaff

LENGTH: 9 miles out and back, with shorter options

ELEVATION: 12,633 feet at top; 9,200 feet at trailhead

DIFFICULTY: strenuous, windy, high elevation

HIGHLIGHTS: isolated volcanic peaks in the Arizona desert, pine and aspen forest

Across the high desert of the Southwest, isolated ranges appear as "sky islands," including the picturesque La Sal Mountains east of Moab, the Abajo and Henry Mountains of southern Utah, and other uplifts. Distinctive among these, the San Francisco Peaks rise just outside of Flagstaff.

Six volcanic cones emerge from the desert plateau that stretches southward from the rim of the Grand Canyon, and Humphreys Peak—at 12,633 feet the highest in Arizona—reaches 3,000 feet above surrounding tablelands. A trail ends at this summit while easier paths cling to ridgelines. Extensive aspen forests cloak lower shoulders and brighten to gold in autumn.

Prepare for intense wind, as these lonely summits catch the brunt of continental blasts. I've weathered 70-mile-per-hour gales here, which means continuing upright is impossible, forcing one to crab-walk or crawl. Lightning hazards are common, especially in the Southwest's monsoon season from July through August; get off the peaks early if threatened!

From Flagstaff, take Highway 180 north for 7 miles to the Snowbowl sign, turn right on Forest Road 516, and wind 7 miles to the northern end of the ski area parking lot and the Humphreys Trailhead.

Blasted by wind in their naked exposure to continental weather, the San Francisco Peaks' uppermost summit, Humphreys Peak, can become unreachable in any normal sense of hiking. Wind speeds of 70 miles per hour on this day defined the limits of the author's ability to stand up.

OPPOSITE: As remnants of volcanoes once erupting through the desert expanse of the Colorado Plateau, the San Francisco Peaks loom high to the north of Flagstaff.

Organ Pipe Cactus National Monument

ARIZONA

LOCATION: Organ Pipe Cactus National Monument south of Gila Bend

LENGTH: 4-mile loop

ELEVATION: 3,050 feet at top; 2,000 feet at trailhead

DIFFICULTY: moderate

HIGHLIGHTS: desert flora and peaks

At Organ Pipe Cactus National Monument, a loop trail in the Ajo Range tours desert gardens of organ pipe cacti, stately saguaro with columnar trunks and uplifted arms, and green-stemmed paloverde whose chlorophyll in twigs complements limited supplies in leaves—all amid rugged volcanic topography. Near the Mexican border, this warm-weather hiking escape has a mild climate all winter. It is best to go from October through April.

Illegal border crossing and drug traffic in the mid-1990s resulted in violent crime and 200 miles of illicit roads being scarred across this desert, closing the monument to public use for 11 years. But after the construction of a 30-mile fence blocking vehicles, the assignment of law enforcement officers, and other precautions, the park reopened in 2014 and has proven safe for visitors.

From Gila Bend on I-8, take Highway 85 south almost to the Mexican border, turn east at Ajo Mountain Drive, and continue to the visitor center and the 21-mile loop road. Park at the Estes Canyon-Bull Pasture Trailhead, with hiking to higher points. When off trail, avoid stepping on the fragile dark crust of cryptogamic soil. Instead, walk on eroded washes, stones, and bedrock.

Among the southernmost mountains, Ajo Peak and other austere summits support an intriguing mix of Sonoran Desert vegetation characterized by spires of saguaro, clusters of organ pipe cacti, and green-stemmed paloverde.

Standing-Up Rocks, Chiricahua Mountains

ARIZONA

LOCATION: Chiricahua National Monument southeast of Willcox

LENGTH: 3 to 7 miles out and back

ELEVATION: 7,307 feet at top; trailhead is about the same

DIFFICULTY: easy to moderate

HIGHLIGHTS: pinnacle formations, pine forest

A series of sky-island mountain ranges emerge from the drylands of southern Arizona, and the volcanic Chiricahua ranks among the most engaging, designated as one of the earlier national monuments in 1924.

With a crowd of rhyolite spires, pinnacles, columns, and curiously balanced rocks hundreds of feet high—all glowing in golden light of southwestern sunsets—the Standing-Up Rocks are reached by trails on slopes that rise from the surrounding desert to catch precious rain and snow.

From the national monument visitor center, the Bonita Canyon Scenic Drive tours the rocky maze. Trails include the 3-mile Echo Canyon loop starting at the Echo Canyon Trailhead and picnic area, and the 7-mile Heart of Rocks Trail looping directly from the visitor center.

From I-10 at Willcox, take Highway 186 southeast to Route 181, and then continue 4 miles to the monument entrance and visitor center.

At high elevations of the Chiricahua Mountains, bunchgrasses and ponderosa pines benefit from snowfall.

OPPOSITE: In the Chiricahua Mountains, trails wind through the pinnacle maze called Heart of Rocks.

Gila River and Mogollon Mountains

NEW MEXICO

LOCATION: Gila National Forest north of Silver City

LENGTH: 13-mile loop

ELEVATION: 6,320 feet at top; 5,620 feet at trailhead

DIFFICULTY: easy, but with stream crossings

HIGHLIGHTS: sheer-wall canyons, large cottonwoods, desert river

With the Southwest's wildest river as the centerpiece, the Gila was one of the first wilderness areas safeguarded by the Forest Service when the revered wildlife biologist Aldo Leopold championed its protection in 1924. Several branches of the river drain the Mogollon Mountains. Combined with four other contiguous uplifts, the Gila ranges constitute the largest contiguous block of mountain terrain in New Mexico.

A fascinating loop trail begins near ancient ruins designated as Gila Cliff Dwellings National Monument. Just east of it, at the TJ Corral Trailhead along the West Fork Gila, the Little Bear Canyon Trail aims north, ascending gently over a saddle separating the West and Middle Fork basins.

After descending to the Middle Fork, hike upstream 2 miles to Jordan Hot Springs and then return downstream, or turn right at the Middle Fork and descend 7 miles, crossing the diminutive stream 32 times. At common low levels the fords are easily waded, but if water levels are rising or rain is forecast, return to the TJ Corral Trailhead. Downstream on the Middle Fork, sheer walls of red sandstone rise while impressive cottonwoods shade the bottomlands. The trail emerges at a visitor center above the West Fork-Middle Fork confluence. From the highway intersection there, go right for a short road walk back to the TJ Corral Trailhead.

The green-up following midsummer monsoon season is especially beautiful, though take care to avoid flashy high water during rainstorms.

From Silver City, take Highway 15 (West Fork Scenic Byway) north for 43 miles to the turnoff for the Forest Service/Bureau of Land Management visitor center, but continue on the main road 1 more mile to the trailhead on the right.

The Gila River Loop Trail descends the gentle gradient of the Middle Fork beneath towering sandstone cliffs and through bottomland sycamore forests.

SIERRA NEVADA

Aligned north-south on the east side of California, the Sierra Nevada impress all who come within sight of the celestial peaks. America's first famous wildlands preservationist, John Muir, adopted the Sierra as his own, calling it the "Range of Light." The mountains extend 400 miles as the ultimate granite batholith—an underground molten mass that hardened into coarse crystalline rock and then seismically arose to the heights now known, and it is still rising. In the southern Sierra, 14,505-foot Mount Whitney (the latest U.S. Geological Survey measurement) reigns as America's highest peak outside Alaska. An astounding 500 Sierra Nevada summits top 12,000 feet.

Unlike other ranges outside Alaska, the Sierra run long and lofty as a continuous uplift with high passes but no low skyline breaks for most of their length from Lake Almanor in the north to the Tehachapi Mountains' east-west intersection in the south. The west side slants up from foothills that begin as grasslands, thicken with chaparral, and, at 3,000 feet, green into what many consider the world's most picturesque coniferous forest. In contrast, the east side is a fault block veering up precipitously as the longest continuous front of steep terrain in America.

John Muir was right: no other range dazzles with such a display of mountain magic. The exquisite light of the Sierra—even tainted by the tailpipes of urban and agricultural California—shines warm and gold as it reflects from whitish granite; from golden trunks of cedars, sequoias, and pines; and from transparent lakes and streams that dot and thread the highcountry.

Where spared of logging, conifers populate parklike settings amid clusters of azalea, all elegant with backdrops of granite cliffs, misty waterfalls, and drifted snowbanks piling to record depths. An aggregate of 86 feet fell in Donner Pass in the winter of 1982–83. By spring, the upper western slope typically sees 12 feet of consolidated snowpack, offering the best springtime skiing anywhere and a reservoir for the rivers that serve urban and agricultural California. However, pernicious dry years and the long-term consequences of climate change are making this supply uncertain and imperiled.

In winter, fearsome storms humble the heartiest shoveler of snow, yet even then the Sierra weather brightens seductively between storms with intervals that can last weeks or even months in distressingly frequent modern droughts. While the highcountry whines with its share of mosquitoes in early summer as snow melts, dry conditions after July and throughout autumn in this Mediterranean climate mean fewer late-season bugs than in many other high ranges. Autumn is precious with cool nights, intense light, vivid colors that enrapture, and afternoon warmth that's balmy late into the season.

Public land accounts for two-thirds of this range, and national park and wilderness designations protect a greater percentage of mountain country here than anywhere else, thanks to a strong conservation movement in California. America's longest and second-largest swath of designated wilderness areas extend nonstop for 145 miles and 2.4 million acres along the Sierra Crest. Here lie 4 of only 16 wild areas in the United States outside Alaska with a 10-mile or larger radius from any road. But because western foothills are mostly private, builders truss up new homes there at breakneck rates—all subject to intensified fire danger in the age of global warming. Even without wildfires, smog from the urban and agricultural maw of the nation's most populous state fans upslope like a teargas bomb, and while per capita air pollution has been reduced, population continues to double every 60 years, with a murky haze persisting. Even so, these mountains have no comparison for their brilliant appeal to hikers.

Pacific Crest Trail, Sierra Nevada

LOCATION: Donner Pass southward through Mount Whitney

LENGTH: 350 miles point to point, with many shorter hikes possible

ELEVATION: 14,505 feet at top; 7,088 feet at Donner Pass

DIFFICULTY: strenuous, high elevation, epic length possible

HIGHLIGHTS: incomparable mountain scenes

The Pacific Crest Trail (PCT) traverses the backbone of this legendary range, and many hikers choose it as America's single most spectacular long-distance route. A full expedition through the Sierra Nevada easily fills a month or more.

North to south, a few highlights include the Desolation Wilderness west of Lake Tahoe, Yosemite National Park's backcountry, granite expanses of wilderness, groves of massive conifers, cascading streams, high passes with views to wonderlands of peaks, snowfields lingering through summer, a few remnant glaciers, dozens of gemlike lakes, and a finale cresting the summit of Mount Whitney—the highest peak in 49 states. Hikers going the distance arrange food drops near roads: typically Echo Lake at Highway 50, Sonora Pass, Tuolumne Meadows, Mammoth, Bishop, or less convenient side-trail access to another pass or two. Some of these require significant detours, each memorable.

Many hikers prefer shorter segments with stellar connecting trails. Popular sections tour Yosemite, Thousand Island Lake, the Mammoth area, the backcountry west of Bishop, Sequoia and Kings Canyon National Parks, and Mount Whitney.

For those who want to go even farther, the full 2,650-mile PCT continues through alluring mountains both north and south of this High Sierra section. Also popular, the 210-mile John Muir Trail from Yosemite Valley to Mount Whitney shadows and overlaps much of the PCT through the High Sierra.

Snowpack usually covers large lengths of the trail in early summer, obscuring portions of the route, with navigation by landmarks in some areas until July. Mosquitoes follow, but they subside as the snow's moisture dissipates, making late summer

PREVIOUS SPREAD: At first light, a full moon shines over the Palisade Crest—a prized view near the beginning of the North Palisade Trail.

With snow lingering in July, the Desolation Wilderness west of Lake Tahoe challenges early season hikers. Pyramid Peak accents the background on the right.

Banner Peak (on the right) and
Mount Ritter reign at the Sierra Crest
above Thousand Island Lake south
of Yosemite National Park.

OPPOSITE: Ornate volcanic horns
decorate the route of the Pacific Crest
Trail north of Ebbetts Pass while
an afternoon storm approaches.

and early autumn perfect with their deliciously mild weather. Southern passes are decidedly higher than northern ones and thus retain snow longer in spite of their decreasing latitude, making north-to-south travel better. Early season travelers should carry ice axes for snowbound passes, which can be steep and hazardously encrusted. Hikers should acclimatize— another reason to travel north to south. Conversely, most thru-hikers attempting the entire PCT launch in the south to avoid an even harsher springtime in the North Cascades and to get an early jump on the hot drylands of Southern California, though this forces them onto treacherous snowfields of the highest Sierra early in the season.

A permit is needed for this most classic of western long-distance hikes, and demand is high.

Apply early to the agency where your trip begins: the National Park Service or Forest Service.

Black bears can be troublesome, especially in the Yosemite and Mount Whitney areas, where bear-proof canisters are required. Water must be filtered or treated. Finally, a significant shuttle is needed for these point-to-point epics, but bus service is possible along Highway 395 on the east side of the mountains. Guidebooks detail the entire route; see the Pacific Crest Trail Association and other sources.

Popular access points are Donner, Echo, Carson, Ebbetts, and Sonora Passes in the north; Tioga Pass Road in Yosemite; Mammoth; Piute or Bishop Passes outside Bishop; and Kearsarge Pass and its trailhead above Independence (Highway 395).

Mount Whitney via New Army Pass

LOCATION: Inyo National Forest, Sequoia National Park

LENGTH: 38 miles one way, plus side trips

ELEVATION: 14,505 feet at top; 10,000 feet at Horseshoe Meadow Trailhead

DIFFICULTY: strenuous, very high elevation

HIGHLIGHTS: highest peak in 49 states, granite wonderland, lakes

This route summits the highest peak in 49 states, traverses vast expanses of the southern Sierra Nevada, visits groves of ancient foxtail pines, edges shimmering granite-rimmed lakes, and offers access to some of the most extreme and starkly beautiful mountain monoliths in America.

This is a near-loop that doesn't quite close; a car shuttle is needed, or a portion of the trip can be done out and back. The option covered here starts south of Lone Pine with a drive up to the Horseshoe Meadow Trailhead. From there, hike north to Cottonwood Lakes and then west over New Army Pass. Here a cross-country side trip directly north makes for a relatively easy ascent of 14,042-foot Mount Langley, with views of the highest Sierra and a vertical eyeful as long and sheer as one is ever likely to see. This side trip also provides an extreme summit experience likely in total solitude, while the Whitney summit will no doubt be a social affair.

Back on the New Army Pass Trail, continue west to the Pacific Crest Trail junction and turn north to Crabtree Meadow at Mount Whitney's western base. If time allows, put this mother of all mountains on hold and walk farther north, as the Sierra's backbone is one of a kind, otherwise difficult to reach, and stunning for the lover of high exposure. Trailside and off-trail excursions lead to Wallace Lake, Wales Lake, majestic Tunnabora Peak, and any number of granite enclaves, lakeshores, and high perches.

Returning to Crabtree Meadow, and with a bit more acclimatization under your belt, set out for the Whitney summit. This west side is far less

Mount Whitney veers into the blue at sunrise, seen from the Alabama Hills above Lone Pine and on the way to the Whitney Portal Trailhead. The east-side summit trail hides to the left.

FOLLOWING SPREAD: Summer storm clouds gather over Tunnabora Peak in the Sierra Nevada north of California's Mount Whitney.

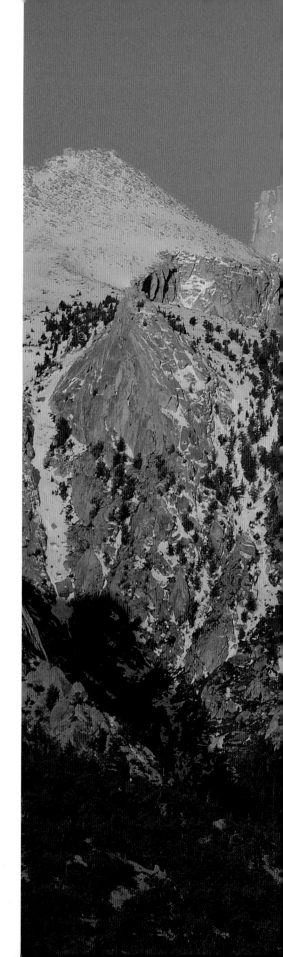

steep than the east slope. Switchbacks ramp to Whitney's theatrical ridgeline, followed by a pinnacled moonscape northward onto the mounded summit and the walk-up mountaintop of a lifetime.

Descend via the Mount Whitney Trail and its own remarkable sequence of lakes, forests, streams, and masterpieces of granite landscaping to Whitney Portal Road curving back down to Lone Pine.

Some hikers may be able to rush through the highest elevations without pain or altitude complications, but a few days at the initial trailhead and then a slow pace as elevation accumulates is a good idea. Sun exposure is likewise extreme in this land of little shade. And the bears are beyond annoying. Bear-proof canisters are required by the Forest Service; if you don't own them, rent them in Lone Pine. Once, having more food than fit in my canisters, I ended up on a midnight trek to food lockers at Crabtree after a bear returned again and again, seen only in moonlight and persistently trying to snag my small counterbalanced cache.

A permit to climb the extremely popular Mount Whitney is needed from Inyo National Forest for overnight and day use, and quotas fill early. Be ready with a backup plan for other Sierra Nevada entry points and trails—nearly all are stellar in their own way.

From Lone Pine, drive west on Whitney Portal Road 3 miles, turn left on Horseshoe Meadows Road, and climb 22 miles to the high-elevation trailhead. For the Whitney Portal Trailhead at 8,400 feet, continue driving west from Lone Pine.

For those targeting only Mount Whitney, the direct round trip from the Whitney Portal Trailhead is 21 miles climbing 6,000 feet. While the length is not extreme, the altitude and gradient are. Most people approaching from the east side need two days to acclimatize, overnighting 6 miles up at Trail Camp; reservations are required and in limited supply.

Elizabeth Pass

LOCATION: Sequoia National Park east of Wolverton

LENGTH: 26-mile loop, including 9 miles off trail

ELEVATION: 11,000 feet at top; 7,250 feet at trailhead

DIFFICULTY: strenuous, significant mileage off trail

HIGHLIGHTS: extreme high-granite landscape, lakes, wilderness

High granite peaks serrate much of the Sierra's 400-mile crest, but especially in the southern half from Yosemite to the Kern River. Hundreds of hikes beckon, including multiple routes in Sequoia National Park.

For this one, start at the Wolverton Trailhead south of the Lodgepole visitor center and walk east, bearing left to Heather, Aster, and Pear Lakes (6.2 miles). This trek alone is good, but more awaits for hikers competent in off-trail routing.

From Pear Lake, embark eastward off trail through a wonderland of walkable granite to Moose Lake and onward. Arc northeast toward Elizabeth Pass, which is on the Great Western Divide, separating the Kings-Kaweah basins to the north and west from the Kern River basin to the east and south.

Intercept an established north-south trail crossing Elizabeth Pass and take it southwest to Lone Pine Creek and west to Bearpaw Meadow, and then follow the High Sierra Trail west for 11 miles back to Wolverton. A topographic map and compass are needed for this trip, as are a backcountry permit from Sequoia National Park, bear-proof canisters, and high-elevation acclimatization.

From Visalia, take Highway 198 to Three Rivers and continue onward to the Wolverton Trailhead.

The moon rises over Lion Rock in the Sequoia National Park backcountry west of Elizabeth Pass.

OPPOSITE: From a granite perch near Elizabeth Pass in Sequoia National Park backcountry, heights of the Sierra Nevada stretch northward.

South Fork Kings River Loop

LOCATION: Kings Canyon National Park east of Fresno

LENGTH: 46-mile loop

ELEVATION: 11,979 feet at Glen Pass; 5,053 feet at trailhead

DIFFICULTY: strenuous

HIGHLIGHTS: cascading streams, lakes, granite highcountry, towering peaks

The upper Kings River basin, entirely within Kings Canyon National Park, offers some of the Sierra's most exquisite terrain—a bit wetter and greener than the starker expanses of granite highcountry to the south.

Begin at Zumwalt Meadow—at the road's end east of Cedar Grove—and hike up the foaming South Fork Kings River. At Bubbs Creek turn right, and at the Pacific Crest Trail go left. Mount the radical divide of Glen Pass, continue north, and then turn west to descend Woods Creek and the South Fork Kings past Mist Falls and back to Zumwalt.

This is some of the Sierra's finest grandeur on a loop taking four days or so with no need for a car shuttle. Precautions apply regarding bears, water filtration, and summer thunderstorms. Get a permit early from the national park for this popular hike.

The route can be stretched for point-to-point epics north, taking out at Florence Lake, or south to Mount Whitney and Lone Pine, or east over Kearsarge Pass to Independence, or east via the less-trod, less-convenient Baxter, Sawmill, and Taboose Passes connecting via obscure gravel roads to Highway 395.

For the South Fork Kings Trailhead from Fresno, take Highway 180 east. In Kings Canyon National Park, bear north on 180 to Cedar Grove and continue to the road's end.

At the South Fork Kings River headwaters, known as Upper Basin, clouds gather at sunrise.

North Palisade Glacier

LOCATION: Inyo National Forest west of Big Pine

LENGTH: 23 miles out and back

ELEVATION: 13,000 feet at top; 7,900 feet at trailhead

DIFFICULTY: moderate, then strenuous to the glacier

HIGHLIGHTS: monumental peaks, the Sierra's largest glacier

A three-day hike on the southeast side of the Sierra Nevada offers a scenic ascent of Big Pine Creek and surreal views of Temple Crag and North Palisade—the third-highest peak in the Sierra Nevada and home to the range's largest glacier, though, like all others, it's disappearing.

From the Big Pine Creek Trailhead, hike uphill, staying right to ascend the North Fork of Big Pine Creek (the South Fork is good, too, with access to the trail-free base of Middle Palisade and its vertical drama). At 6 miles, the trail skirts slopes above Second Lake with views directly into Temple Crag's ornate, vertical, and otherworldly rise, and also spellbinding scenes across the valley to the soaring North Palisade and its sister peaks: Sill, Polemonium, Thunderbolt, and Winchell.

Another 1.5 miles lead to the base of North Palisade's glacial runoff stream. A user trail, stairway-steep, climbs 1 mile to Sam Mack Meadow. From there, launch off trail up the scree-riddled ridge route to the left. Another mile or so leads to the massive moraine of loose rock at the base of the glacier. Proceed, or mount the ridgeline of boulders on the left between the glacier and Mount Gayley. Views of the glacier open at the top of the lateral moraine. Care must be taken with rock-stepping; the moraine material is unconsolidated, and multiton rocks can tip with a footstep. Return, or carefully scramble down the moraine to the glacier above its ice-end lake. Assiduously avoid going near the lake's upper end or sides, as boulders and glacial ice randomly plunge into it—a severe hazard invisible from above.

With crampons, or with special care on a warm day's softened snow, one can walk another mile up the glacier to where a final pitch ends with an eyeful of gaping bergschrund and where casual climbing ends. This largest glacier so far south in

Aptly named, Temple Crag fills the view adjacent to North Palisade.

OPPOSITE: The monumental North Palisade—the third-highest peak in the Sierra Nevada—presides on the left while the square-topped Thunderbolt Peak occupies the center after a late-season storm in May dumped a foot of snow on the highcountry.

the United States is one of only two in the Sierra that still exhibit active glacial traits with crevasses, bergschrunds, perched rocks, and moving ice. The North Pal's one-of-a-kind experience in the Sierra is quickly disappearing. Backpacking permits are needed from Inyo National Forest.

Take Highway 395 to Big Pine, turn west on Glacier Lodge Road (the lodge is gone), and continue 10 miles to the trailhead. Other nearby hikes venture up the South Fork of Big Pine Creek with off-trail routes to Middle Palisade, Norman Clyde Peak, and magnetic views to the jagged Palisade Crest.

Piute Pass

LOCATION: Inyo National Forest southwest of Bishop

LENGTH: 12 miles out and back, with longer trips possible

ELEVATION: 11,423 feet at top; 9,350 feet at trailhead

DIFFICULTY: moderate

HIGHLIGHTS: highcountry, peaks, lakes

The trail up the North Fork Bishop Creek to Piute Pass is an extraordinary yet accessible route for summer hiking or winter travel on snowshoes or skis. Trails and off-trail routes westward from the pass continue to granite-rimmed lakes and then drop into Piute Canyon of the South Fork San Joaquin River, with limitless hiking beyond.

Unusual in the southeastern Sierra, this trail offers ramped access (with a few steep sections) compared to other routes that pose severe avalanche possibilities in winter and spring. If tempted to plot a loop trip then, don't. Or be aware that alternate routes back down the eastern escarpment to the north (Pine Creek Canyon) and the south (Lamarck Col, and farther at Bishop Pass) present serious avalanche hazards. Permits for backpacking are required; call Inyo National Forest.

From Bishop on Highway 395, take Line Street west. Ascend Bishop Creek Road toward Lake Sabrina, but turn right just before it and continue to the end.

Bishop Creek Road offers paved access to more spectacular and concentrated high-mountain hiking possibilities than any other road in America. Eleven trails lead directly into exhilarating highcountry from trailheads perched at 9,000 feet. Options include multiple paths from South Lake, Lake Sabrina, and North Lake. Summertime access here also crosses the Sierra Crest to favorite sections of the John Muir and Pacific Crest Trails, including the revered Evolution Valley.

Backcountry skier Steve Schmitz traverses the west side of Piute Pass. A superb summer hiking route and relatively safe skiing destination—considering the extreme steepness of other passes—the Piute route opens to views here at the San Joaquin River headwaters.

Yosemite Valley

LOCATION: Yosemite National Park

LENGTH: 1 to 10 miles out and back

ELEVATION: 7,000 feet at top; 4,000 feet at valley floor

DIFFICULTY: mostly easy, some strenuous

HIGHLIGHTS: waterfalls, cliffs, river frontage, Yosemite Valley

Many people consider Yosemite Valley the scenic climax of America. And who can argue? From John Muir onward, this place has impressed visitors as an idol of natural beauty with its elegant composition of waterfalls, the country's tallest sheer walls of granite, garden-like artwork of forests and meadows, and exhilarating open space mixed with welcoming recesses among rocks and trees—the ultimate in the dual qualities of prospect and refuge. It is a landscape that's both exciting and comforting at once. While the hikes here do not climax on mountain peaks—those lie above the valley and its encircling rim of granite—any tour of the most beautiful mountain landscapes in America would not be complete without a walk through this memorable valley.

An intricate and extensive network of trails can be strolled by hikers of all abilities, in all seasons. Three must-do walks, at some time in your life, include the following:

➤ **Yosemite Falls:** Paved and crowded trails venture to the base, while a steep, strenuous, worthwhile climb ascends the left side to the

In Edenic Yosemite Valley, California black oaks anchor their roots in meadows while ponderosa pines darken lower slopes that veer up to imposing granite walls.

OPPOSITE: April snowstorms whiten exposed ledges while Yosemite Creek's spray freezes on chilled rock at one of the tallest waterfalls worldwide.

top. Yosemite Creek's combined falls have been called the third highest in the world. At the base, throngs of visitors by the busload can be avoided early and late in the day.

➤ **Merced River to Vernal and Nevada Falls:** At the head of the valley, a paved trail climbs to Vernal Falls, while continued stairstepping reaches the breathtaking brink of Nevada Falls. Though crowded, this trail is a must-do for waterfall aficionados.

➤ **Leidig Meadow:** At the heart of the valley, just west of Yosemite Valley Lodge, a flat path circumnavigates the sublime beauty of this meadow with stunning cliffs all around, including nearby El Capitan, considered the largest cliff face on earth. Come at sunset or daybreak—alone and quietly—and spend some time for the ultimate meditation, surrounded at those hours by both beauty and near-solitude in this otherwise busy place.

Most people can walk the lower reaches of these and other trails, and a fit hiker can continue on heart-thumping climbs to the valley rim. Routes can be traveled separately or linked throughout the valley. Continuous free bus service obviates the need for cars in Yosemite's one-way road system, which carries heavy traffic up one side of the valley and down the other—a loop that renders the center of the incomparable valley into the world's most beautiful median strip.

For the most transformative experience, visit Yosemite Valley on weekdays and during shoulder seasons. April and October are my favorite times.

From Central California's I-5, take Highway 120 east to the Big Oak Flat Road entrance to the park and onward to the valley. Farther south, take Highway 140 to the El Portal entrance. From the east, take Highway 395 to Lee Vining and go west on 120, which is closed from November to July.

Half Dome Summit

LOCATION: Yosemite National Park

LENGTH: 16 miles out and back

ELEVATION: 8,842 feet at top; 3,900 feet at Happy Isles Trailhead

DIFFICULTY: extremely strenuous

HIGHLIGHTS: bird's-eye view of Yosemite Valley, unique and exciting climb

Distinctively shaped and descriptively named, the granite monument of Half Dome rises 4,800 feet from Happy Isles at the head of Yosemite Valley. It's the signature landmark of a park that many consider the scenic culmination of the entire national park system, and the climb to Half Dome's summit may be the most extreme "walk-up" that many hikers will ever do. A dazzling bird's-eye view of Yosemite Valley, directly below, awaits, along with panoramas to Tenaya and Merced Canyons and eastward to the Sierra Crest.

This strenuous day hike is best expanded to a two- or three-day outing by backpacking via the Merced River—with its own attractions of Vernal and Nevada Falls—to the Little Yosemite Valley camping area. On the next day, climb Half Dome, then return to the valley's Happy Isles Trailhead afterward or on the third day.

Following the long lead-up and its challenging elevation gain, the final thrilling 400-foot pitch up the granite-crowned east side of Half Dome is possible via steel cables, installed by the Park Service, from Memorial Day through Columbus Day. With boards placed crosswise for foot traction, the railing-like cables allow capable hikers to ascend the extended exposure otherwise unsafe without rock-climbing skills and roped belay. Bring traction gloves, available in gardening stores, for a secure grip.

This climb is no place for the acrophobic or the unfit. Stay away whenever thunderstorms and lightning threaten—most likely on summer afternoons. Avoid hazards by summiting early in the day—another reason to backpack to Little Yosemite Valley and ascend from there at dawn.

Permits for the Half Dome climb are required from Yosemite National Park, and the daily quota of 300 fills; reserve early and expect a lineup of pilgrims at the cables during prime hours. To avoid crowds, go on weekdays, at daybreak, and in early autumn. A separate permit to camp at Little Yosemite Valley is not required if you have a Half Dome or other relevant wilderness permit.

The cable-aided climbing route up the concave mound of Half Dome, with exfoliating slabs of granite, is ascended here at daybreak by hikers nearing the top.

OPPOSITE: The incomparable view from the summit of Half Dome telescopes to a lone hiker perched 4,800 feet above Yosemite Valley.

For a fabulous option or add-on—which evades the Half Dome permit requirement but not the wilderness permit—hike from Little Yosemite Valley toward Half Dome but angle northeast 4 more miles to Clouds Rest (9,926 feet) and its commanding view 1,000 feet down to Half Dome's summit and onward to Yosemite Valley in receding miniature. From the Yosemite Valley base at the Happy Isles Trailhead, this 20-mile round trip climbs 6,000 feet.

Grand Canyon of the Tuolumne River

LOCATION: northern Yosemite National Park

LENGTH: 18 to 31 miles out and back, with shorter hikes possible

ELEVATION: 8,619 feet at trailhead; 3,790 feet at bottom

DIFFICULTY: moderate to strenuous

HIGHLIGHTS: granite canyon with high-volume whitewater and waterfalls

In the high runoff of June, a six-foot wave forms at the brink of Glen Aulin Falls in the Grand Canyon of the Tuolumne River.

FOLLOWING SPREAD: Under a rainbow colored by a bright sunrise in the Grand Canyon of the Tuolumne River, early season runoff plunges over California Falls (left). In the Grand Canyon of the Tuolumne River, Ann Vileisis witnesses the power of California Falls during high runoff (right).

Yosemite National Park is full of superlatives, and I regard this trek as America's most exceptional hike through a mountain canyon with waterfalls. At high flows in June, the explosive whitewater and chain of breathtaking cataracts create the most extraordinary hydrologic phenomenon one is ever likely to see.

From the Lembert Dome parking area in Tuolumne Meadows, take the Pacific Crest Trail down the north side of the river. Use caution at fords that may require wading in icy snowmelt early in summer. Explore off trail to the base of the first falls, about 4 miles down, with its backdrop to Cathedral Peak. At 6 miles, another waterfall plunges to Glen Aulin and its commercial campsite with meals and wall tents (reservations are required). The commercial camp's heavy horse traffic, and obvious signs of it, are left behind at this point.

Continue downstream to waterfalls called California, LeConte, and Waterwheel, and past the rapids in between. Return from Waterwheel for a 19-mile round trip, or proceed until almost reaching Hetch Hetchy Reservoir. Then trek up the south side of the canyon to White Wolf Campground and Tioga Pass Road, served by shuttle buses—altogether a 31-mile point-to-point backpack trip.

When Tioga Pass Road first opens, typically in late June, the foaming tumult is most impressive. Midsummer trips appeal differently with hot days, and autumn has its chilly charms, though pesky flies linger here surprisingly late. Permits for overnight backpacking are required.

From Yosemite Valley, drive or catch the bus to Tuolumne Meadows, or approach from the east side via Tioga Pass Road.

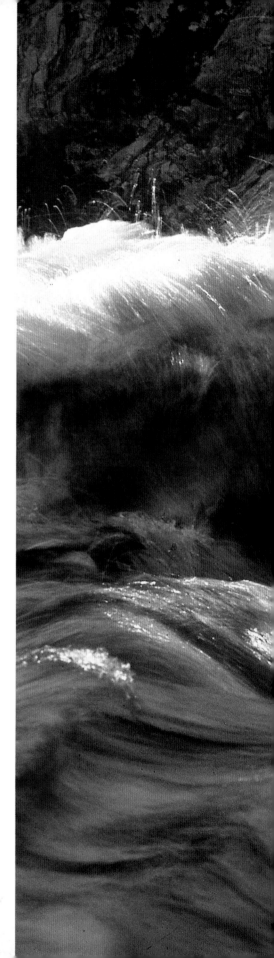

Mount Conness

LOCATION: Inyo National Forest west of Lee Vining

LENGTH: 10 miles out and back

ELEVATION: 12,590 feet at top; 10,087 feet at trailhead

DIFFICULTY: very strenuous, high elevation, short Class 4 climbing pitch

HIGHLIGHTS: summit climb, exceptional mountaineering experience

This monolithic landmark off the northeastern corner of Yosemite National Park offers a climbing adventure that captures the exposure and thrill of a mountaineering ascent but can be done by competent hikers without technical rock-climbing gear after midsummer. A few Class 4 moves, with handholds and a bit of moderate exposure, are required. The entire ascent presents an array of lakes and mountain features, the climb is challenging, and the view from the top is extreme and expansive.

From the Saddlebag Lake Trailhead east of Tioga Pass, hike immediately west on a climber's path toward Lake Alpine, into the pass between Mount Conness to the north and White Mountain to the south, and then northwest toward the summit. A high plateau and distinctive narrow ridgeline curves to the top. While line-of-sight routing to the summit worked fine for me, detailed route descriptions are available in guidebooks.

High elevation can limit the unacclimatized. Beware of bad weather and summer thunderstorms.

From Yosemite Valley, drive east on Tioga Pass Road, or from Lee Vining, drive west on it. East of the pass, turn north on Saddlebag Lake Road, with parking at the end.

Mount Conness glows at sunrise in the glaciated uplands of Inyo National Forest just east of Yosemite National Park. A remnant glacier clings to shaded slopes at the base of the upper walls.

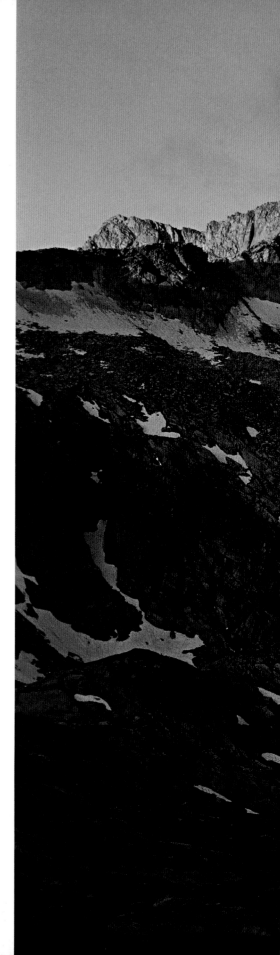

Carson Pass

LOCATION: Sierra Crest east of Jackson

LENGTH: 1 to 10 miles out and back

ELEVATION: 9,585 feet at Elephants Back; 8,652 feet at trailhead

DIFFICULTY: easy to moderate, with harder climbs nearby

HIGHLIGHTS: easy access to meadows, lakes, and peaks

Although this beautiful area might be overlooked among the Sierra Nevada's extravaganza of high-country, the paved highway that crosses the range's backbone here offers some of the easiest access to the crest, and the moderate elevation may not trouble hikers who are not acclimatized. It's also the southernmost pass that's plowed in winter (200 miles of snowbound wildness stretch south to the next road crossing that's open year-round), making Carson an excellent launch for winter and spring-time ski or snowshoe trips. A SNO-PARK permit, available online or at regional stores and outdoor outlets, is needed through May; on weekends arrive early for a spot.

From the parking lot, hike southward on the Pacific Crest Trail. Groves of western white pines and mountain junipers of immense girth open to meadows blanketed with wildflowers in early summer. Hikers can strike eastward from the Pacific Crest Trail for an off-trail ascent of Elephants Back and its panoramic views of the northern Sierra and the Monitor Range and Great Basin Desert.

Other paths drop to Winnemucca and Round Lakes, and also southward to Fourth of July Lake. Rocky routes climb exposed ridgelines of Round Top Peak (10,381 feet) to the immediate south, with scrambling that requires some handholds. If the Carson Pass lot is full, trailheads off Highway 88 west of Carson Pass at Woods Lake Campground and near the Caples Lake outlet also serve Winnemucca and Emigrant Lakes. A separate hike north of Carson Pass connects with steep but easy off-trail ascents to spacious summits of Red Lake Peak (10,063 feet) and Stevens Peak (10,059 feet).

Day hikes and backpacking are both good; for overnights, a permit is required from Eldorado National Forest but should be available. The Pacific Crest Trail here links to longer hikes.

From Jackson, take Highway 88 east to the pass, or from South Lake Tahoe, take 89 and then 88 south and west.

Enjoying the stable conditions, sunny afternoon, and granular corn snow of late springtime, Ann Vileisis cuts telemark turns down the western slant of Carson Pass. As the highest Sierra pass kept open to cars in winter and spring, Carson is a destination for skiers all winter and for hikers after the early summer melt.

OPPOSITE: On the east side of Carson Pass, paintbrush and lupine bloom among sagebrush and ceanothus, filling spaces between granite boulders once deposited by glaciers.

CASCADE MOUNTAINS

Interlocking with the Sierra Nevada in continuous north-south alignment, the stately Cascade Range, 650 miles long, extends from Northern California to British Columbia and beyond. A dozen stratovolcanoes here rank among America's most distinctive mountains, with snowcaps as symmetrical as those drawn by a first grader. And the volcanism is definitely not just a thing of the past. Mount St. Helens, Rainier, Shasta, Hood, and the Three Sisters in Washington and Oregon are among the top seven volcanoes that the U.S. Geological Survey expects to erupt again (the others are in Alaska). But there should be early warning signals of this and, for now, the Cascades' glaciated peaks, combined with emerald forests below and summertime's blue sky above, are to many hikers the ultimate in mountain beauty.

Major Cascade peaks include the towering cone of Mount Shasta in California and the white visage of Mount Hood rising over Portland, Oregon. In Washington, a pyroclastic explosion blew Mount St. Helens sky-high in 1980, reducing its snow-cone profile to a scooped-out hulk of pumice above scorched forests. That volcanic event awoke the nation to the fact that the earth—and especially the Pacific Northwest—is still in the process of being reformed in truly astonishing ways. At 14,410 feet, Mount Rainier reigns as Queen of the Cascades and its highest peak. Beyond, in the North Cascades, volcanic cones intermingle with granite summits and ripsaw ridgelines—together a mountain wonderland whose combined steepness, size, and wildness are challenged by only a few other ranges in the Lower 48.

The sky-reaching Cascade peaks rear abruptly from relatively low elevations. Other than summit and high-flank climbs, much of the hiking is through temperate terrain of enchanted mossy forests—where they haven't been cut over. This mostly means designated wilderness within national forests and a few exquisite national parks.

Some high slopes remain covered by snow or glaciers all year—especially the northern faces. But much of the trail mileage becomes accessible by late spring, except when cold, late-season storms bring snow to low elevations, which is increasingly rare. Precipitation of one form or another is extremely heavy from November to March, light to nonexistent in summer, and mixed in spring and fall—the same Mediterranean climate sequence that graces California, only less sunny and more rainy—altogether making summer and fall a great time to hike in the Cascades.

Mount Shasta

LOCATION: Shasta-Trinity National Forest northeast of Redding

LENGTH: 12 miles out and back for the summit, with other options

ELEVATION: 14,162 feet at top; 6,800 feet at trailhead

DIFFICULTY: very strenuous

HIGHLIGHTS: one of America's most majestic peaks

PREVIOUS SPREAD: Spectacular in views from above and from its flanks, Washington's Mount Rainier emblematizes the Cascade Range: bigger-than-life volcanoes rising in glacier-covered radiance from lowlands surrounding them.

With otherworldly allure, Mount Shasta in Northern California is the second-highest summit in the Cascade Range. The volcanic subsidiary peak, Shastina, accompanies the taller mountain and ranks as the third-highest summit in the range.

Mount Shasta lies near the southern end of the Cascade chain of volcanoes. Gleaming white with snow and ice, this symmetrical monolith rises like an apparition that hardly seems possible from the drylands and forests surrounding it.

For the easiest access, and the most feasible summit route, start at the Bunny Flat ski area west of Mount Shasta City. This is the place for adjustment to altitude by wandering the red-fir forest and timberline meadows for a few days if possible, enjoying mountain vistas everywhere. These, in fact, are some of the choicest views, as you have to stay back a bit to really see the full frame of this glacier-sculpted volcanic monolith. Bunny Flat's easy but intimate exposure to the mountain might even be enough for many hikers. But for the full experience, acclimatize and then take the Avalanche Gulch (John Muir) route up. One day makes for a grueling climb and descent; many people prefer two days. High-elevation hiking and overnight camping permits are required from the Forest Service.

With crumbly pumice underfoot, the route quickly ascends to the Sierra Club's Horse Camp shelter at timberline. Higher, and often snow-bound, Lake Helen is a layover bivouac site. Take warm gear and a stove for melting snow to drink. Crampons and an ice ax are definitely needed, and helmets for rockfall are strongly recommended. In summer conditions, and with crampons and axes, capable climbers will not need to be roped together for safety.

Topping 14,000 feet, this second-tallest summit of the Cascade Range is likely to cause altitude distress to most hikers approaching from low elevations, even after holding at Bunny Flat for a day or two. Many climbers sprint to the summit and

At Mount Shasta's less-visited east side, Hotlum Glacier lies to the right. A hiking route ascends to midelevations via the ridge immediately left of the glacier.

OPPOSITE: With an unmatched chaos of crevasses and jumbled seracs, the surface of Hotlum Glacier can be explored only by teams of experienced climbers taking precautions against falls into gaping voids below. Here climber Nettie Pardue takes in the severe grandeur.

quickly descend to avoid prolonged exposure to headaches and altitude sickness, as I did, but to no avail. Be careful when glissading and trying to rush the return; accidents occur when sliding down snowfields riddled with rocks, not to mention the risk of loosening projectiles onto hikers below.

Heavy snow makes climbing difficult until summer, yet melting makes walking on loose pumice and cinders a slog with an increased danger of rockfall. Mid-May through mid-July is usually best. Dress well; even on this California idol, the weather can turn terrible.

A west-side vent on the stratovolcano formed the subsidiary peak, Shastina. Welded to the big mountain's slope, it tops 12,330 feet and—though

rarely counted—ranks as the third-highest summit of the entire Cascade Range. A fine climb in its own right, Shastina can typically be done without crampons in summer and imposes less altitude stress. From Bunny Flat, proceed as if aiming for Shasta but then veer left (west), cross Casaval Ridge, and traverse to Shastina's east saddle and visible summit.

To reach Bunny Flat, take I-5 to the town of Mount Shasta and drive east on Highway A10 to the ski area parking lot.

Other hikes are possible from various angles around Mount Shasta, though all are more challenging, less visited, and require back-road driving. My favorite is Shasta's northeastern face from the south side of Hotlum Glacier, which presents extreme ice features, including crevasses and seracs found nowhere else this far south. Walking on the glacier any higher than the ice's solid bottom runout is extremely hazardous without an experienced, roped team of climbers. However, the amazing ice display can be viewed from a rocky ridge reached by ascending snowfields immediately to the glacier's south (left side). Be aware, however, that the summit climb from there is difficult and technical—only for experienced mountaineers. Approach Hotlum's base via Route 89 east of McCloud, turn north on Military Pass Road, and go west on Forest Road 42N02 and 42N10. Take a map and *The Mount Shasta Book* by Andy Selters and Michael Zanger.

Permits and a fee for hiking or backpacking above 10,000 feet are required from Shasta-Trinity National Forest. Human waste must be packed out of the Mount Shasta Wilderness. It's easier than most people think—grab free sealable bags at trailheads.

While Mount Shasta is the big fish of the southern Cascades, Mount Lassen—65 miles southward—makes a more doable introduction to the range. At 10,457 feet, it's much lower and easier, and it's the range's southernmost summit. On the southern face, fit hikers can hustle 5 miles from the Lassen Volcanic National Park road to the top and back in half a day.

Upper Rogue River Trail

OREGON

LOCATION: Rogue River-Siskiyou National Forest northeast of Medford

LENGTH: 50 miles one way, with shorter options possible

ELEVATION: 5,394 feet at top; 2,566 feet at bottom trailhead

DIFFICULTY: easy

HIGHLIGHTS: wild river, big trees, volcanic geology

This is one of the best mountain trails along a riverfront anywhere, with waterfalls, swimming holes, enchanting old-growth forest, and a parade of curious volcanic features.

From the Crater Rim Viewpoint north of Crater Lake National Park, a spur trail leads to the Rogue River's origin—a perennial spring sourced in the depths of landlocked Crater Lake 8 miles away. This area burned in 2015, but remains mostly green along the river. Below, and west from the trailhead, the path angles downstream, first on the north side at the rim of a sharply incised pumice canyon 600 feet deep, then descends from the recent burn to shrouded green forests, nearly always in sight or earshot of pure, bubbling waters. Near Union Creek Campground, the entire Rogue disappears into a lava tube and boils underground for 200 feet before bursting into daylight again.

Frequent road accesses make this outing ideal for either backpacking or day hiking, with convenient shuttle by bike or car on the paralleling paved highway—nearby but not intrusively so.

To reach the upper trailhead from Crater Lake National Park's north entrance road, take Highway 230 west for 4 miles to Crater Rim Viewpoint. For day hiking, also use trailheads at Hamaker Campground, Rogue Gorge, Union Creek, Natural Bridge, and Woodruff Bridge. The bottom access is at North Fork Park, west of Prospect. See the Rogue River-Siskiyou National Forest map.

Other outstanding mountain trails along Oregon's Cascade riverfronts follow the North Umpqua, McKenzie, Middle Fork Willamette, Clackamas, and Salmon Rivers. But the Upper Rogue fills a class by itself for its combined beauty, length, geologic features, and deep forest.

The Upper Rogue River Trail follows this stellar Cascade Mountain stream from its headwaters downward for 50 miles. A light snowfall whitens the corridor in winter.

In its passage from the underground outlet of Crater Lake and downward to Cascade Mountain foothills, the Upper Rogue River Trail penetrates deep forests of western hemlock.

Mount Scott

LOCATION: Crater Lake National Park

LENGTH: 5 miles out and back

ELEVATION: 8,926 feet at top; 7,720 feet at trailhead

DIFFICULTY: easy

HIGHLIGHTS: views of Crater Lake, mountain hemlocks, whitebark pines

South of Mount Scott, the Garfield Peak Trail ramps up to heights of Mount Mazama's rim ringing Crater Lake.

OPPOSITE: Mount Scott crowns the eastern horizon seen from Crater Lake. Closer, Garfield Peak rises on the right.

Crater Lake is America's one-of-a-kind caldera. When the bulky cone of Mount Mazama erupted only 6,000 years ago, the void left by the ejected lava settled into a 2,148-foot-deep caldera now partly filled with America's deepest lake. The rim around this 5-mile-diameter disc of intense blue is continuously scenic, and the hike to Mount Scott's fire tower offers views west to this geologic and lacustrine wonder, north to the lightning-rod pinnacle of Mount Thielsen, and south to the Klamath Basin, Mount McLoughlin, and distant Mount Shasta. This may be the easiest hike to a major Cascade summit, and it makes a great introduction to Oregon's Cascade Mountains.

From Highway 62 in Medford, drive northeast to the turnoff for Crater Lake—Oregon's only national park. Climb toward the rim, but short of it

turn east on the rim's loop road and proceed counterclockwise 10 miles to the Mount Scott Trailhead. Or, from the park's north entrance, drive up to the rim and then go left (clockwise) 13 miles.

Closer to the lake, 8,054-foot Garfield Peak has terrific views reached with a 3-mile round-trip walk directly from Crater Lake Lodge's perch at the rim. The road to the lodge is open all winter, while East Rim Road to Mount Scott remains closed until mid-June or so.

For unique mountain charm, from the northern shore of the lake at Cleetwood Cove, take the 1-mile trail down 700 vertical feet to the water and catch a tour boat—reservations are recommended from June to September—to Wizard Island. This perfectly shaped minivolcano arose as an aftermath within the sunken caldera. Disembark and walk 5 miles round trip to the summit. The boat will wait for you.

After the 7-mile-wide caldera of Mount Mazama collapsed and created Crater Lake, additional volcanic eruptions formed Wizard Island within the watery depths. In summer, hikers can summit the volcanic island after taking a short boat ride.

South Sister

LOCATION: Deschutes National Forest west of Bend

LENGTH: 12 miles out and back

ELEVATION: 10,358 feet at top; 5,450 feet at trailhead

DIFFICULTY: very strenuous

HIGHLIGHTS: major Cascade climb, sweeping panorama, glaciers

The Three Sisters—South, Middle, and North—crown the Cascade crest midway through its north-south alignment in Oregon, and the South Sister—the third-highest mountain in the state—is Oregon's highest nontechnical summit climb. The loftier Mounts Hood and Jefferson demand far more skill, experience, and equipment.

Pack lots of water, lunch, foul-weather gear, poles, and gaiters for the loose rock that will otherwise annoyingly fill your shoes as if someone was pouring stones into them.

North of the Devils Lake Trailhead, the Cascade woods will yield to barren volcanic terrain. Hike north to Moraine Lake, which alone makes a good destination without the relentless gradient on loose cinders to come. The lake can also be a final destination if clouds obscure the summit—little point in going there then—or if thunderstorms threaten.

Otherwise, follow a beaten path up the southern face of the immense domed mountain, passing between Clark Glacier on the left and Lewis Glacier on the right. The final pitch up volcanic rock and dusty ash ends at the rim of a distinct crater containing Teardrop Pool—vividly turquoise with summer's melt.

Beware of bad weather, springtime avalanches, exhaustion, and dehydration on this taxing adventure. An option is to backpack to timberline, camp, and then day hike to the top. Go early in the morning, and consider early summer or autumn to avoid crowds and heat. A limit on daily numbers is being considered; contact Deschutes National Forest for that status.

From Bend, take Cascade Lakes Highway (46) west for 28 miles. Beyond Sparks Lake, park at the Devils Lake Trailhead.

Without the steep incline, the low-lying Green Lakes Trail hugs the east side of the Three Sisters and makes for great hiking. Start just west of Soda Creek Campground near Sparks Lake. For big mileage, a 48-mile loop trail encircles the combined South, Middle, and North Sisters and reveals them like nothing else does; start at the Lava Lake Camp Trailhead.

The Middle and North Sisters cap the Cascade Mountain horizon, seen here from the glacier-sculpted flanks of the taller South Sister.

Jefferson Park

OREGON

LOCATION: Willamette National Forest east of Salem

LENGTH: 11 miles out and back

ELEVATION: 5,880 feet at top; 4,080 feet at trailhead

DIFFICULTY: strenuous

HIGHLIGHTS: Cascade view, meadows, lakes

Mount Jefferson is a sharply eroded lightning rod east of Salem and a highlight of the Cascades. While the summit is for mountaineers relishing both glacial and near-vertical challenges, Jefferson Park's popular high basin of meadow-ringed lakes offers breathtaking views to the mountain's prominent rise southward. Among three access routes, the Whitewater Trailhead, east of Detroit Reservoir, requires the least driving, offers the easiest trail, and features a close-up view of the charismatic volcanic plug.

From Salem, drive east on Highway 22 to Detroit and onward 10 miles to the gravel Whitewater Road (Forest Road 2243) on the left. Take it for 8 miles to the trailhead. After hiking 1.5 miles, stay right and continue to the Pacific Crest Trail and Jefferson Park. Fabulous views await there, and even more from the ridge rising north of the park's seductive meadows and lakes. Day hike northward on the Pacific Crest Trail 900 vertical feet up to Park Ridge, which shelters a few awesome and less-buggy campsites if you carry water.

Finding Whitewater Road closed because of recent fires, I took Breitenbush Lake Road farther north, but it became a rough, rocky minefield for my van; I ended up walking the last few miles to the trailhead.

Snow can linger in Jefferson Park to July. Early summer camping is buggy but delightfully flowered. Autumn offers exquisite, crowd-free, chilled nights. No campfires are allowed here, and tenting near lakes must be on established sites.

From Park Ridge, the view south to Mount Jefferson is considered one of Oregon's premier mountain scenes.

Mount Hood to Columbia River

LOCATION: Mount Hood National Forest east of Portland

LENGTH: 36 miles one way, with shorter hikes possible

ELEVATION: 6,000 feet at top; 220 feet at bottom

DIFFICULTY: moderate, extended downhill backpack trip

HIGHLIGHTS: Mount Hood, waterfalls, hike from timberline to nearly sea level

As the state's highest peak, spectacularly dressed in forests, glaciers, and underlying volcanic features, Mount Hood—seen here above Timberline Lodge—is emblematic of Oregon.

Mount Hood is the Cascades' crown in Oregon. At 11,249 feet, the state's highest peak rises prominently as a showy white backdrop in views from Portland. The elegant landmark's high slopes can be reached via paved road ending at Timberline Lodge—an attraction for the architecture alone. From there, any number of mountain strolls begin without prelude in the brilliant meadows and high forests and rise with increasing drama onto snowdrifts, volcanic rockfall, and ridgelines of pumice angling up toward the summit. Any pretense of casual climbing ends on glacial slopes where a gaping crevasse is eventually encountered; only equipped and experienced teams of mountaineers should press farther.

Wandering Mount Hood's timberline slopes is euphoric, but the epic outing here is from Timberline Lodge down to the Columbia River— the only place south of Alaska where one can trail walk from timberline to virtually sea level (though not to the ocean; the Columbia is tidal for 140 miles to Bonneville Dam).

Starting at the lodge, walk just upslope and to the west and watch for the Pacific Crest Trail (PCT), which may be snowbound into July. Trend left on the PCT, or at your closest approximation of it, and wrap around the southwestern flanks of the mountain, soon dropping below timberline and switchbacking down to a crossing of Zigzag River. This and other fords may run high in early summer. Continue to the PCT's Ramona Falls intersection and take a detour up to the remarkable spray onto truncated end grain of columnar basalt. Continue north on the PCT to a gravel road and

With its stratospheric rise above lower country, Mount Hood breeds depthless snowstorms and gleams in fresh winter dress above Timberline Lodge.

OPPOSITE: Robust spring-flows from porous volcanic rock feed Eagle Creek. The hike from Mount Hood to the Columbia River follows this stream for 7 miles as the finest timberline-to-near-sea-level hike south of Canada. Much of the area burned in the wildfires of 2018.

Lolo Pass at mile 12 of the trip, and then continue northward via the PCT to Indian Springs at mile 23. Take a crucial left off the PCT and onto Eagle Creek Trail and descend its length. Much of it burned in 2018. The lower 6 miles pass seven major cataracts, starting with Tunnel Falls and the trail's fantasy passage behind it. Eagle Creek emerges near the Columbia River just east of Bonneville Dam, only 200 feet above sea level.

To reach the top, drive east from Portland on Highway 26 past Sandy and turn left to Mount Hood and Timberline Lodge. For the bottom, follow I-84 east from Portland to exit 41 and angle south to the Eagle Creek Trailhead—a national forest pass is required. Avoid leaving cars overnight; break-ins plague the Columbia River Gorge, where persistent crime is incongruent to the beauty of the place.

Also epic, a 41-mile route circumnavigates Mount Hood with a gross gain of 8,600 feet; from Timberline Lodge, take summertime's paved pathway uphill, go left on the PCT, and follow signs for the Timberline Trail.

Mount Rainier

LOCATION: Mount Rainier National Park southeast of Seattle

LENGTH: 93-mile loop, with shorter sections

ELEVATION: 6,750 feet at Panhandle Gap; 2,330 feet at low point at Ipsut Creek

DIFFICULTY: very strenuous

HIGHLIGHTS: extraordinary views, meadows, high forests, glaciers

Mount Rainier is likely to rank in any hiker's book as one of the most extraordinary peaks in America, if not the top one. Its massive bulk soars skyward as an incomparable dome of snow and ice. Twenty-six glaciers remain breathtaking, for now, even in the age of global warming.

Just a casual walk is well worth the visit; drive to the rambling log lodge at Paradise on the south side of the mountain, and then wander the slopes at timberline. The mountain is beautiful with heavy snow cover, but hiking around its flanks is best in late summer.

For total immersion and one of the classic mountain hikes in America, embark on the Wonderland Trail—a well-named 93-mile circumnavigation of the awesome mountain. This backpacking adventure of a week or more takes the hiker to countless views of the peak, glacier edges, plunging streams by the dozen, miles of wildflower meadows, and wind-sculpted forests deepening into dark old-growth trees and green riparian lushness. A whopping gross climb of 22,000 feet is more than summiting Alaska's Denali. Stay at designated campsites—there are 21 in all.

From Seattle, take one of various highways and then either 410 to the north side of Mount Rainier National Park or 706 to the south side and Paradise Inn. Also a superb hike, and far less intimidating, the High Skyline Trail climbs above ornate Nisqually Glacier and loops 6 miles with 1,700 feet of gain; start on the north side of the Paradise parking lot. Backpacking permits are required from Mount Rainier National Park.

Starry green foliage of vine maples and a fallen western red cedar contribute to an ecosystem of rich complexity along streams radiating from Mount Rainier.

OPPOSITE: Queen of the Cascade Range, Mount Rainier in springtime remains lacquered in deep snow upslope from the Paradise Inn.

Glacier Peak and Lyman Lake

LOCATION: Mount Baker-Snoqualmie National Forest north of Leavenworth

LENGTH: 53-mile loop

ELEVATION: 7,500 feet at Spider Gap; 2,900 feet at trailhead

DIFFICULTY: strenuous and long

HIGHLIGHTS: views of Glacier Peak, glacier walking, highcountry, meadows

The North Cascades are the supremely rugged, glaciated mountain mass rising north of the Skykomish and Wenatchee Rivers and marching nonstop into Canada. This is one of the most continuously high, wild mountain refuges in America south of Alaska. Many trails penetrate the Shangri-la of peaks and valleys, but deep access to this wilderness is difficult by any standard.

Hidden in this uplifted wonderworld, Glacier Peak is the Cascade Range's only towering stratovolcano that cannot be seen from any road. It's a challenge just to lay eyes on the 10,541-foot summit, which—owing to deep snowfall and latitude—looks way higher. A phenomenal route beckons to the determined hiker, and it includes far more than views of this elusive ice-armored volcano.

Prep for a rigorous outing of five days or more. From Leavenworth, drive on Highway 2 northwest 16 miles, and then north on Route 207. Continue on the gravel Chiwawa River Road northwest to its end at the Trinity Trailhead.

The hike begins with a 10-mile, 2,100-foot climb to Buck Creek Pass east of Glacier Peak. From there, carry water on a spur trail running 2 miles west to Liberty Cap with elegant views of the peak—definitely worth bivouacking for the sunset and sunrise. Back at Buck Creek Pass, the main trail continues north 7 miles to the Pacific Crest Trail (PCT), which has taken a long, separate roadless route around the west side of Glacier Peak. Go right on the PCT and continue 3.4 miles, and then turn left and continue 4.5 miles to campsites with sublime views of the glacier-clad volcano's reflection in Image Lake.

Glacier Peak is the only outsized stratovolcano of the Pacific Northwest that cannot be seen from a road. Here the elegant mountain rises behind Image Lake.

Looping back to the Glacier Peak Trailhead, the Phelps Creek Trail descends through brilliant meadows to Chiwawa River Road.

OPPOSITE: Runoff from the Lyman Glacier pools into its uppermost meltwater lake on the Glacier Peak-Lyman Lake loop.

Return back east 4.5 miles to the PCT, follow it 1.5 miles north over Suiattle Pass, and then go right and over Cloudy Pass for 2.3 miles to the striking wild beauty of Lyman Lake. Turn south and continue 2.2 miles, climb trail free for 2 miles over the snowfields and firm glacial ice of Spider Gap, and then descend 8 miles down Phelps Creek Trail and back to the car.

More demanding, a 96-mile loop encircles Glacier Peak with a gross climb of 15,500 feet for savvy hikers. This can be split into a 52- or 44-mile segment with a car shuttle, similar to Mount Rainier's Wonderland Trail but minus a lot of people.

Mount Baker

LOCATION: Mount Baker-Snoqualmie National Forest east of Bellingham

LENGTH: 8 miles out and back, with shorter and longer hikes possible

ELEVATION: 6,000 feet at top; 4,800 feet at trailhead

DIFFICULTY: easy

HIGHLIGHTS: views of a Cascade peak, glaciers up close, meadows

Glacier clad and freshened by snowfall, Mount Shuksan rises in the muted morning light of the North Cascades near Mount Baker.

FOLLOWING SPREAD: October clouds bearing the first snowstorm of the year brew in the background as Ann Vileisis returns from Mount Baker. Peaks of the Canadian border dominate the horizon line (left). Mount Baker might be considered the perfect snow cone, with wind-sculpted hemlocks embellishing the foreground (top right). A hearty grove of mountain hemlocks—charismatic arboreal giants of the western peaks—survives the ages at its craggy outpost protected from wind, fire, and deep snowdrifts on the flanks of Mount Baker (bottom right).

It's hard to imagine the Cascades getting better and better as you go north, but they do. Mount Baker is one of America's most extraordinary seldom-seen mountains. Rain or snowstorms obscure this out-of-the-way landmark for much of the year, and even in summer many attempts to visit are foiled. But a clear day here is one to be remembered.

Highway 542 winds eastward from Bellingham, eventually ascending the North Fork Nooksack River. The pavement passes the Mount Baker ski area and emerges with eastward views to Mount Shuksan—a masterpiece of glaciated scenery in its own right and one of America's most-celebrated mountain photos, right up there with the Maroon Bells and Grand Teton. The road ends at a timberline parking lot immediately north of Mount Baker's gleaming supernatural rise.

Views to Mount Shuksan await with a path to the east, while to the west and south a welcoming trail emerges from the trees with explosive views to Mount Baker's northeastern face—as severely glaciated as any mountain scene in America.

The trail continues in a traverse and ridge walk toward the ice-clad monolith rising point-blank ahead. Adventurous hikers can go to the ice itself. Climbing beyond is only for mountaineers prepared for glacial travel and extreme crevasse hazards.

Traveling to Mount Baker is not worth the drive without a suitable weather report; on many days, there is little chance to even see the mountain, let alone hike to its glacial base. But on a clear day, few mountain experiences can compare.

COAST RANGE

Rising abruptly from the Pacific Ocean, the Coast Range stands with intriguing variety as the nation's longest mountain chain. In mountaineering hype and vacation planning, this uplift at the continent's edge might typically take a back seat to the Rockies, Sierra, and Cascades, but listen: North America's Coast Range continues with few interruptions for 5,000 miles from the Baja Peninsula in Mexico to Kodiak Island in Alaska. It's like driving from San Francisco to Miami and then up the Atlantic coast to Philadelphia and having it *all* be mountains!

Southern California has peaks topping 10,000 feet, while typical summits northward reach 1,000 to 3,000 feet through Washington—which is not much compared to other western ranges. But remember, these mountains come straight out of the ocean at elevation zero rather than curving upward from perched valleys, so the relief is often similar. And farther north, in Canada and Alaska, peaks abruptly aim skyward owing to unimaginable tectonic forces of the Pacific Plate colliding directly with the North American Plate. This confrontation of irresistible force versus immovable object grinds rocks together, pushes summits up, and creates a chaos of ridges and valleys undergoing constant flux with earthquakes that humble anything in their way.

A product of such geological and climatic mandates, these mountains harbor an intricate diversity of life in their forests, chaparral, grasslands, alpine heights, glacier edges, tidal fringes, and geographically entangled transition zones of biological fascination found nowhere else.

Dozens of coastal subranges link like spliced ropes end to end. In Southern California, the Peninsular Ranges (referring to the Baja Peninsula but also mountains similarly aligned north of it) include the Palomar Range east of San Diego, which leads northward to the Santa Ana Mountains veering up from the Los Angeles suburbs and eastward to the skyscraping San Jacinto Mountains. These ranges tie into the Transverse Ranges that track an east-west axis due to a strange kink in the San Andreas Fault attributed to the Great Basin's continental drift and geologic stretch westward. They include the Tehachapi, San Bernardino, San Gabriel, Santa Monica, and Santa Ynez Mountains.

The twin San Rafael and Sierra Madre then bend in parallel tandem northwest, merging into the Santa Lucia Range of Big Sur fame along California's photogenic Central Coast.

North of San Francisco Bay, grassy or wooded ridgelines top the oceanfront and continue through Oregon and Washington. Though they are related and adjacent to the coastal complex, for the purpose of this book I separate the Klamath-Siskiyou and Olympic Mountains into separate hiking sections owing to their size, distinctive geology and geography, and hiking opportunities.

Not ending but rather picking up steam, the Coast Range resumes in Canada on Vancouver Island and the British Columbia mainland and continues through the mountain-and-forest archipelago of southeastern Alaska, where hundreds of conifer-clad islands reveal only the tops of mountains rising from a depthless sea. East of the tidal inlets, truly awesome peaks reign—some springing from sea level to 14,000 feet in one leap, as if Mount Whitney or the Sawatch Range of Colorado were plucked up and redeposited at the ocean's edge with no intervening topography. The Coast Range of Alaska is also covered under a separate section of this book.

The whole length of the Coast Range rumbles with earthquake faults, including the infamous San Andreas in the south, the direct subduction of the Juan de Fuca Plate against the North American Plate in Oregon and Washington, and the mountain-making fractures of Alaska with their vastly intensified force.

California's seductively balmy coast boasts a Mediterranean climate of dry weather much of the year but has wet winters. This pattern continues northward, but with the dry phase progressively muted while the rainy season intensifies. As a result, the north gets far less sun and a whole lot of rain, but still in seasonal patterns. In fall and winter, the mountaintops of the Lost Coast of Northern California, along with the Olympic Peninsula and coast of Alaska, see more precipitation than any other areas in the United States outside Hawaii (on the island of Kauai, Mount Waialeale dwarfs all others with 450 inches a year—the second-wettest place on earth).

Seasonal rains notwithstanding, the Coast Range weather—unlike other mountains of the West that are known for climatic extremes—is tempered by the sea and its relatively uniform temperatures and humidity. This makes hiking possible year-round, given the limitations of wet days from San Francisco northward.

Another plus for hikers here: with its lower elevations, most of the Coast Range requires no acclimatization by visitors who otherwise need time for adjustment. And still another advantage: with intensifying heat, wildfires, and smoke that's increasingly prevalent through much of the summer in wide swaths of the interior West, the coast beckons with typically clear, clean skies even when inland locations choke on smoke. With a chain of overflowing cities from San Diego and Los Angeles to San Francisco and Seattle sited literally at their bases, these ranges are, in many ways, the people's mountains of America.

Mount San Antonio

LOCATION: Angeles National Forest north of Claremont

LENGTH: 6 miles out and back

ELEVATION: 10,064 feet at top; 7,802 feet at trailhead

DIFFICULTY: strenuous

HIGHLIGHTS: views to Southern California mountains, high-elevation forests

Surprising to many people, mountains dominate the landscape of Southern California just outside the cities. In fact, the greater Los Angeles area is bordered by the nontropical world's longest urban-wildland interface—a continuous perimeter of 680 miles where development stops abruptly, for the most part, at rugged terrain rimming the basin, which is literally made of alluvial soil eroded from the mountains and redeposited over the eons by rain, streams, and mudslides that overpower any object or investment in their path.

One of the highest points along this geographic theater is Mount San Antonio (Mount Baldy) in the San Gabriel Mountains of Angeles National Forest. While trails ascend the Southern California ranges from lower Los Angeles Basin elevations—and are big draws for urban hikers—the most direct route to Mount San Antonio is from the Mount Baldy ski area. From spring through fall, walk up the ski slopes to the ridgetop and then take user paths and the Devil's Backbone Trail northwest along the high divide to Mount Harwood and farther to Mount San Antonio. Return the same way or, if you want to be more adventurous, take opportu-

nistic paths and trails down the southern face of San Antonio leading to Baldy Bowl Trail, passing near San Antonio Falls and on toward the Manker Campground Trailhead—0.3 miles up the road from the campground and just a short distance from the ski area parking lot where you started.

This hike climbs 2,200 feet, but from the summit down to the Los Angeles Basin's valley floor is 9,000 feet—vertical relief outdone in few areas of America. Even Mount Whitney, at 14,505 feet, rises from a 4,000-foot valley, so the relief here in Southern California is comparable. Reflecting the elevation, windswept pines—including limber, ponderosa, Jeffrey, and lodgepole—look more native to the Rocky Mountains than to typical Southern California vegetation. The summit also offers views of the San Andreas Rift Zone—the famous geologic lynchpin of the West Coast the whole way to Cape Mendocino south of Eureka (not to be confused with the town of Mendocino farther south).

From Los Angeles, take I-10 east to Claremont, go north on Mills Avenue to Mount Baldy Road, turn right, and ascend San Antonio Canyon to the end at the Mount Baldy ski area.

PREVIOUS SPREAD: The Coast Range continues with only a few low-lying breaks for 5,000 miles from the Baja Peninsula in Mexico to Kodiak Island in Alaska. Here a happy couple climbs to the overlook on the north side of Tennessee Cove in the Marin Headlands of California.

Just outside the Los Angeles urban area, Mount San Antonio crowns the San Gabriel Mountains. The high-elevation climate breeds wind-sculpted limber pines like it does at the heights of the Rocky Mountains.

Backbone Trail

LOCATION: northwest of Santa Monica

LENGTH: 67 miles point to point, with many shorter hikes possible

ELEVATION: 3,111 feet at top; 25 feet at Point Mugu Trailhead; 2,040 feet at Sandstone Peak Trailhead

DIFFICULTY: moderate to strenuous

HIGHLIGHTS: ocean views, sycamores, mild winter weather

Bumping into the nation's second-largest megalopolis, the Santa Monica Mountains rise as the western terminus of the Transverse Ranges, which surprisingly track east-west just north of Los Angeles. With balmy weather likely in winter, guaranteed in spring, and still sweet in summer and fall, this accessible, compact range tempts any hiker who nears.

A network of paths spanning the Santa Monica Mountains National Recreation Area link together as the 67-mile Backbone Trail, with its eastern terminus in Will Rogers State Historic Park north of Highway 1—an urban edge only 25 miles from downtown Los Angeles. The mountains' wildest reaches lie to the west. So close to the city's bustle, one section of trail amazingly stretches 16 miles without a road crossing. The National Park Service does not recommend thru-hiking of the trail because campsites are not adequate at this time. Linked day hikes for the full distance are possible.

Starting in the west, at Point Mugu State Park, hikers can ascend Sycamore Canyon, named for the stream bottom's magnificent trees with artistically mottled bark, and top out at Boney Mountain—12 miles one way. Sandstone Peak, the highest in the Santa Monica Mountains, is served more immediately by a loop trail from the Circle X Ranch public parking lot. Rocky outcrops tower over canyons veining a colorful and textured mosaic of fire-adapted chaparral. The mountains dip into the sea and then reemerge, still in view, as the Channel Islands, enchanting on a clear day from such distance. Other Backbone Trail attractions are the wilds of Malibu Creek State Park, with vertical peaks, refreshing streamfronts, and inviting sycamore bottoms.

Much of this route burned in 2018. Check with the Santa Monica Mountains National Recreation Area for trail conditions.

From Los Angeles, take the Pacific Coast Highway (Route 1, or the PCH) west and north to roads that ascend the Santa Monica Mountains' multiple ocean-bound canyons. For Point Mugu, continue west on 101 toward Oxnard. For Boney Mountain, take the PCH past Leo Carrillo State Beach to Yerba Buena Road (Little Sycamore Canyon) and go north. For Malibu Creek State Park, take Malibu Canyon Road north from the PCH.

Sandstone Peak caps the boulder-riddled heights of the Santa Monica Mountains fronting the Pacific Ocean west of Los Angeles.

Cone Peak

LOCATION: Los Padres National Forest north of San Simeon

LENGTH: 4 miles out and back, or 12 miles one way from sea level

ELEVATION: 5,155 feet at top; 3,855 feet at Coast Ridge Road Trailhead; 100 feet at Kirk Creek Trailhead

DIFFICULTY: strenuous

HIGHLIGHTS: views to the Pacific Ocean and Santa Lucia Mountains

Cone Peak is the highest mountain rising directly out of the ocean south of Canada, its summit only 3.4 miles from the sea. Nacimiento-Fergusson Road winds to a saddle south of the peak. From there, a rough dirt road of 5 miles is followed by a 2-mile trail gaining 1,400 feet. This hike is best done as a duathlon by mountain biking the first 5 miles and then walking.

Within Los Padres National Forest, this is the ultimate mountain outing along the famed Big Sur coastline—the breathtaking collision of Santa Lucia Mountains and sea. The range starts north of San Simeon and continues to Carmel.

Cone Peak offers sweeping views of the coastline and also the Santa Lucia Mountains' impressive entanglement of peaks and canyons reaching north, south, and inland to Junipero Serra Peak, which is likewise reached by a summit trail. At 5,862 feet, this is the Santa Lucia Mountains' highest point, though unlike Cone Peak, Junipero Serra Peak sits back 11 miles, the ocean hidden.

Accessible along Nacimiento-Fergusson Road, Cone Peak's lower slopes of grass, chaparral, sculptural oaks, and redwood groves bloom and green up vividly in springtime and can be explored trail free with steep, grassy walks from pullouts where the paved road switchbacks radically toward the Coast Range saddle. Beware of ticks, especially in spring, and poison oak all year.

To get to Cone Peak, take Highway 1 along the coast north to Gorda, and then continue 6 more miles to Mill Creek. Just beyond, turn east on the paved Nacimiento-Fergusson Road and its 7-mile climb to the saddle. Park there and bike north on the dirt Cone Peak Road, or drive the rough surface for 5 miles to the summit trail on the left. But parking space is limited.

Higher than any other summit on the Pacific edge south of Canada, Cone Peak accents the skyline of the Santa Lucia Range, seen here from the south along the Big Sur coastline.

For an epic Santa Lucia experience, hike from peak to sea. The Vicente Flat and Kirk Creek Trails link Cone Peak Road with the seashore at Kirk Creek Campground. The upper trailhead hides along Cone Peak Road about 3 miles north of Nacimiento-Fergusson Road. However, this edgy experience will likely be a bit overgrown with chaparral where brush overwhelms maintenance efforts. Dress well—poison oak is grabby—or stay away if your reactions are severe.

Another good Santa Lucia trail, at the northern end of the Big Sur coast, climbs from Bottchers Gap to Ventana Double Cone. This 30-mile out-and-back trail rises to the rock-walled Ventana Double Cone, with an eye out to sea, though trail conditions were poor as of 2018 owing to storm erosion and the chaparral's postfire vigor. From Garrapata State Park, drive south 3 miles, turn east on Palo Colorado Road, and wind uphill 8 miles to the Bottchers Gap Campground and Trailhead (there is a fee).

All Big Sur roads and trails are subject to periodic closures due to storms, landslides, fires, and earthquakes. It's a bit of a wonder that Highway 1 was ever built at all, and a full cost accounting would be shocking. Check with the California Department of Transportation (Caltrans) or Los Padres National Forest for current conditions of roads and trails.

Ocean fog penetrates inland at the flanks of Cone Peak.

Marin Headlands

LOCATION: Golden Gate National Recreation Area north of San Francisco

LENGTH: 21 miles one way, with shorter hikes possible

ELEVATION: 2,572 feet at top; lowest elevation is sea level

DIFFICULTY: easy to moderate

HIGHLIGHTS: ocean and mountain views near San Francisco

The Marin Headlands may be America's most spectacular mountainous open space at the edge of a major urban area. I can't think of more delightful near-city hiking anywhere. Times spent wandering these trails in springtime are the days of heaven.

You can literally walk from San Francisco to this network of fire roads and trails leading to enchanting crescent beaches, commanding vertical headlands, rolling ridgelines with breezy oceanic views, and old-growth redwoods sequestered in Muir Woods National Monument. The terrain is mountainous but accessible, and the vegetation is surprisingly open and grassy. Little forest blocks the view until reaching the invitingly shady groves on Mount Tamalpais, while the headlands also lack the scratchy thickets of chaparral that typify slopes of Southern California. Making it extraeasy, buses serve the trailheads.

My favorites here are the Pacific Rim trails between Tennessee Cove and Muir Beach, with their dizzying drops and awesome ocean views. Fire roads wide enough for social outings serve as the arterial network. Narrower paths connect these roads and lure walkers to exceptional outposts.

While most hikers will serially select any number of day hikes here, it's possible to trek 21 miles from San Francisco northward to Stinson Beach through mountains the whole way. This Bay Area exploration, which seems longer than it is, can begin by walking across the Golden Gate Bridge—a bit

In springtime, cow parsnip blooms in white near the Coast View Trailhead north of Muir Beach while Mount Tamalpais tops the horizon.

OPPOSITE: Hiker Marietta Smith explores a side trail spangled with coastal tidy tips, California poppies, and lupine on the south side of Tennessee Cove at the Marin Headlands.

FOLLOWING SPREAD: The Marin Headlands stand vertically at a cape south of Muir Beach while San Francisco gleams as a white city in the distance.

deafening, plus frightening for the acrophobic, but a unique experience in its own right, especially for bridge aficionados. On the north side, a trail from the walkway cuts *under* the bridge's north abutment.

Covering the southern half of the Marin Headlands, routes from the Golden Gate Bridge to Muir Beach total 10 miles, topping out at 800 feet. Then, after a 2-mile northbound interlude on car-crowded Highway 1 or via Muir Beach's curly residential streets, angle east on the Coast View Trail. This trail links with other routes to the top of Mount Tamalpais at 2,572 feet.

Additional trails connect northward to Stinson Beach via rolling grasslands and oak groves, with exhilarating views back to San Francisco and out to sea. Combining all of this for an extended trip of several days is one of America's great near-urban backpacking adventures. Intimate perches, secluded groves, and off-trail enclaves can be found along the way. Fires are prohibited. Formal backcountry campsites are available with reservations; check online with Golden Gate National Recreation Area, Muir Woods National Monument, and Mount Tamalpais State Park. Water is limited but available at Muir Beach and Mount Tamalpais. Hikers can catch a bus at Stinson Beach for the return shuttle.

Winter hiking here is good when it's not raining; springtime is intoxicatingly green and flowered; summer is fine but often foggy, especially in the morning; and autumn is glorious and starts to green with the first rains. Overall, this location has some of the best year-round mountain walking in America. Expect a lot of company on weekends, but a festive spirit of joy seems to be shared by all.

Drive north on Highway 101 and take the first exit north of the Golden Gate Bridge toward Fort Cronkhite. Or, 5 miles farther, exit on Highway 1 northbound and shortly turn left to the popular Tennessee Valley Trailhead. Or, after Highway 1's tortuously winding hill climb and plummet back to sea level, take the left turn to Muir Beach or continue to Stinson Beach. See Golden Gate National Recreation Area maps.

Lost Coast and Sinkyone Wilderness

LOCATION: north of Fort Bragg, south of Eureka

LENGTH: 56 miles one way, with shorter hikes possible

ELEVATION: 2,500 feet at top; begins and ends at sea level

DIFFICULTY: moderate to strenuous

HIGHLIGHTS: wilderness seascape, headlands, old-growth forests

The Sinkyone Wilderness stretches northward to Chemise Mountain.

FOLLOWING SPREAD: The Lost Coast of Northern California begins at the mouth of the Mattole River and runs south, linking with the Sinkyone Wilderness for the greatest mountain hike along the West Coast of the United States.

This Northern California hike is the premier extended mountain trek along the Pacific coast in America. Trails and beaches intersect for memorable backpacking, with an unmatched kaleidoscope of ocean views, headlands, mossy forests, colorful wildflower meadows, crashing surf, and intricate tidal pools. Olympic National Park's coastline is likewise a classic backpacking destination, but the terrain on Washington's coastal plain is not mountainous, while this geography is emphatically so.

Two distinct segments—the Lost Coast in the north and Sinkyone Wilderness in the south—can be done separately or combined for an epic week.

By walking north to south, the wind is at your back—no small advantage here at America's western limits, where nothing breaks the trans-Pacific gales this side of Alaska or Japan. Start at the mouth of the Mattole River. It's worth the winding drive just to visit the wild outlet—one of California's few sizable rivers with a completely natural mouth unmarred by jetties, harbors, or riprap. From there, the Lost Coast section of this hike stretches southward for 24 miles along the beaches at the narrow toe of the King Range, stewarded by the federal Bureau of Land Management. A few rocky capes require low tide for safe passage and perhaps a well-timed sprint between waves. Take a tide table (though local crests seem to vary a lot) and a change of socks!

Nearing an ill-fated subdivision called Shelter Cove, at ground zero of the San Andreas Fault, the flatness of Lost Coast beach walking ends because impassable headlands veer southward. Trek uphill on the paved Shelter Cove Road, and, 4 miles from

the beach, turn south to the Hidden Valley area, where a woodland trail commences.

From there, wild forests blanket ocean-edge mountains and the trail repeatedly bridges Pacific-bound streams, all within the enchanted woodlands of Sinkyone Wilderness State Park. Old-growth firs and redwoods crowd the path as it winds up tributary enclaves, tops ridgelines or headlands, and pitches down to the next stream, whimsically emerging at pocket-size beaches where you might see any combination of barking seals, grunting sea lions, bugling elk, spouting whales, and hosts of birds and intertidal life. (Mountain lions prowl as well; on my last trip, I stumbled on a warm elk kill and, seeing the carnage remaining to be eaten, chose to not linger and to look as large as possible as I departed.) Southward, the Sinkyone section emerges at Usal Campground and its rough dirt road.

Beware of ticks in springtime, poison oak, and high tides, and prep for rain in springtime and a chilling fog in summer. Tempting as it is, do not camp near tide line; erratic waves are treacherous along this coast. Swim only with extreme care and avoid all steep beaches and stream mouths, which cause undertows along deceptively appealing waterfronts.

For the northern terminus, drive west from Highway 101 at the South Fork/Honeydew exit in Humboldt Redwoods State Park. Steer patiently westward over the Coast Range's 23 serpentine miles to Honeydew, and then onward via Smith-Etter Road to the Mattole's mouth. For the southern access, take Highway 1 north from Fort Bragg, followed by scarcely noticeable Rockport. Just after the road angles inland, take the hairpin turn left onto the dirt Usal Road—dicey when wet—and continue 4 miles to the Usal Trailhead and Campground. For the hike's midpoint at Shelter Cove, take Highway 101 to Redway and go west on wiggling Briceland and Shelter Cove Roads. Beware of leaving cars overnight, especially at this midpoint. Adequate maps are the ticket for all approaches.

Prairie Creek Redwoods

CALIFORNIA

This hike offers one of the best trails anywhere through majestic groves of redwoods topping 300 feet. A gentle climb over the westernmost Coast Range topography leads to an Edenic canyon bedecked in ferns, favorite pastures of the world's largest species of elk, and campsites just a stroll from Pacific whitecaps. It's also the top hike combining redwoods and oceanfront, and it's the redwood coast's primary backpacking opportunity for an easy two to three days.

The 7-mile Irvine Trail from the Prairie Creek visitor center tours redwoods and Fern Canyon and ends at Gold Bluffs Beach and Campground, with an easy car shuttle. But longer options await without the need for a second car. A loop of 15 miles via the coastal Ossagon Trail makes an excellent backpacking trip, as does the 11-mile loop using the Irvine and Miners Ridge Trails while camping at the Miners Ridge walk-in site. Overnight permits are required and in heavy demand; contact Prairie Creek Redwoods State Park. Simply day hike these routes if you have to switch to Plan B. Maps are available at the visitor center.

Expect morning fog in summer, and be alert to its sun-warmed hour of clearing: that's when streaks of light are aimed between the branches and down to hikers' humble presence beneath the towering trees. Summertime temperatures here peak in the 60s when interior California bakes at 105 degrees—the ocean is a big air conditioner.

Take Highway 101 south from Crescent City or north from Arcata, exit on the Newton B. Drury Scenic Parkway, and at its southern end find the Prairie Creek visitor center and trailhead. The park has 75 miles of trails, with car camping at Elk Prairie among redwoods or at Gold Bluffs Beach on the coast.

The coast redwoods are the tallest trees in America. They thrive on summer fog, which is prevalent along California's North Coast owing to prevailing winds and the resulting ocean currents and upwelling of deep, cold seawater.

Often seen in Prairie Creek Redwoods State Park, Roosevelt elk graze near Gold Bluffs Beach.

OPPOSITE: Trails of Prairie Creek Redwoods State Park cross a low uplift of the Coast Range and link with Fern Canyon and its Pacific-bound runoff.

Humbug Mountain

LOCATION: Humbug Mountain State Park south of Port Orford

LENGTH: 6-mile loop

ELEVATION: 1,756 feet at top; 50 feet at trailhead

DIFFICULTY: strenuous but short

HIGHLIGHTS: old-growth conifers, ocean views

Humbug Mountain is the highest peak rising directly from the sea on the Oregon coast and the finest northwestern mountain hike fronting the ocean. From the parking lot, a trail zigzags through old-growth Douglas firs, western hemlocks, grand firs, bays, and bigleaf maples of massive girth, hoary with moss and lichen. East- and west-fork options top out in 3 miles.

The west-side trail is steeper, with more sunshine on clear days. About halfway up, a window through tall trees opens for a view north to Port Orford and Cape Blanco—the westernmost point in 48 states except for the tip of the Olympic Peninsula. Don't expect a big vista on top; a vigorous fir forest encroaches on the summit's shrinking grassy bald.

Take Highway 101 north from Gold Beach or south from Port Orford to Humbug Mountain State Park and the trailhead, which is directly across 101 from the campground.

For a complementary eyeful while you're there, walk seaward from the campground and under the Highway 101 bridge to a magnificent beach at the base of Humbug Mountain, where the greenery and gradient match the island of Kauai. Also, the 360-mile Oregon Coast Trail passes through this park. Much of it follows roads, but a 26-mile section nearby, Gold Beach to Brookings, is nearly all off road and absolutely splendid.

Humbug Mountain, whose indigenous name is translated as "salmon cheek," peaks at 1,756 feet—the tallest summit rising directly from the ocean on the Oregon coast.

OPPOSITE: The 3-mile trail switchbacking to the top of Humbug Mountain offers a tour of ancient Douglas firs, western hemlocks, and grand firs.

KLAMATH AND SISKIYOU RANGES

Though inseparably adjoining the coastal mountains—and sometimes considered part of them—the combined Klamath and Siskiyou Ranges are a 250-by-80-mile-wide jumble of severe topography extending from the Coast Range at the Pacific edge eastward to the Cascades, and once geologically connected to the Sierra Nevada, effectively linking these four ranges into a continuous uplift unmatched in the United States for its aggregate mass of mountain length and width.

This terrain boasts the most biologically diverse forests in the West. Here grow the world's largest variety of conifer species—38 according to botanist John O. Sawyer—plus more endemic plants than anywhere in the United States except the biological hot spot of southern Appalachia. The International Union for the Conservation of Nature (United Nations) designated these mountains a distinguished "area of global botanical significance." Meanwhile, a fabulous array of wild rivers carves this terrain beneath forested peaks.

In California, America's most populated state, and in southwestern Oregon, the population density is five people per square mile—surprisingly less than in Idaho or Montana. Hikers are not likely to encounter crowds, or in many cases even a single soul, which makes the appeal of the Klamath and Siskiyou Ranges all the stronger.

Thompson Peak

LOCATION: Shasta-Trinity National Forest northeast of Arcata

LENGTH: 20 miles out and back

ELEVATION: 8,920 feet at top; 4,200 feet at low point

DIFFICULTY: strenuous

HIGHLIGHTS: old-growth forest, waterfall, glacier

The Salmon Mountains—often called the Trinity Alps—have backcountry similar to the northern Sierra Nevada, with granite peaks, lakes, and coniferous forests, making this subrange the most popular one for hikers in the Klamath-Siskiyou region. Most trailheads are accessed from Highway 3 in eastern reaches and from spur roads north of Highway 299. The popular Canyon Creek Trail explores California's second-largest wilderness area.

Less known, and lightly traveled, the trail to Grizzly Lake and onward to Thompson Peak offers a tantalizing backpack trip with big trees, a magnificent waterfall at the lake's outlet, and highcountry embracing the coastal mountains' only remaining glacier south of the Olympic Peninsula.

The first 3 miles of this hike trek southward over the Salmon River-Trinity River divide and down to Grizzly Creek. Turn left and hike east (upstream) 5 miles to Grizzly Meadows and the trail's end. Camp there and then day hike onward, or continue trail free up the steep boulder scramble to the left of the waterfall. This leads to Grizzly Lake, with off-trail ascents to high meadows at the base of Thompson Peak and its small receding glacier, whose years are tightly numbered due to global warming.

For this distant, remote trailhead northeast of Arcata, take a map and drive on Highway 299 east. Go north on Highway 96 to Somes Bar, turn east and ascend the paved but cliffhanging Salmon River Road, and at Forks of Salmon go right and up the South Fork to its East Fork. Bear right again, continue about 3 miles to Schoolhouse Flat, turn right, and proceed south on a dirt road that climbs 3 miles to the China Gulch (Grizzly Creek) Trailhead.

PREVIOUS SPREAD: Jeffrey pines cling tenaciously to life along the Kalmiopsis Rim Trail of Oregon's Kalmiopsis Wilderness, where recent fires have burned. Whetstone Butte dominates the middle ground.

Still thawing in May, Grizzly Lake hides in the shadows of the Trinity Alps.

OPPOSITE: The highest summit in the Trinity Alps, Thompson Peak also harbors the only remaining glacier of the Coast Range south of the Olympic Mountains, though the ice and snowfield are rapidly receding.

Castle Crags

LOCATION: southwest of Mount Shasta

LENGTH: 6 miles out and back, with shorter routes possible

ELEVATION: 4,800 feet at top; 2,600 feet at trailhead

DIFFICULTY: strenuous

HIGHLIGHTS: granite crags, Mount Shasta views

An extraordinary bang for the buck where the Klamath Mountains' eastern edge abuts the Cascade Range, the Castle Crags point skyward just off of I-5. Granite peaks and domes make believable the geologists' surprising narrative that these mountains were once connected to the Sierra Nevada. Highlighting a network of trails, the crags route rises 2,200 feet to the thrilling base of Castle Dome with point-blank views to the other crags, north to Mount Shasta, and west to the Klamath Range. Just the view from Vista Point at the end of the road is worth the short drive off I-5. The Pacific Crest Trail (PCT) also traverses Castle Crags State Park for 8 miles, including views of the crags and the Sacramento River Canyon.

From I-5 south of Dunsmuir, take the Castle Crags exit, go 1 mile to the state park, and take Vista Point Road to its end and the trailhead.

While you're here, there are a few other worthwhile Klamath-Siskiyou outings as well. For paved road access and woodland walks, consider the PCT south of Ashland, Oregon, easily reached from exit 6 (Mount Ashland) off I-5. With a longer but still paved byway, the PCT dramatically crosses the Klamath Mountains at the head of the Salmon River basin. From I-5 at Yreka, take Highway 3 southwest to Etna, turn right on Sawyers Bar Road, and wind up to Etna Summit-Salmon River Pass. Hike north on the PCT with views to the Marble Mountains or south to the Russian Wilderness.

For those who don't mind a difficult approach, the Young's Valley-Clear Creek Trail, best with autumn's cooldown, offers remote perspectives to this region's remarkable coniferous forest through some of the Klamath-Siskiyou's most rugged terrain. From Highway 199 east of Crescent City, drive

Granite cliffs and domes rise in Castle Crags State Park, where the Klamath Range merges with the Cascade Mountains southwest of Mount Shasta.

to the upper Smith River basin, and, about 3 miles before (west) of the summit, turn south on Knopki Creek Road. Follow its roughness south 16 miles to the Young's Valley Trailhead. The trail's first 3 miles overlay a scruffy, abandoned mining road, but then a narrow path descends Clear Creek toward the Klamath River with superb groves of incense cedar, rare Port Orford cedar, and other conifers. Reached via side trail, Devil's Punchbowl is the Siskiyou Mountains' outstanding glacial cirque.

OPPOSITE: Rare Port Orford cedars and incense cedars tower over the upper Clear Creek Trail of the Siskiyou Mountains south of the remote Young's Valley Trailhead.

At the height of the Siskiyou Mountains in southern Oregon, a Shasta red fir reaches for the sky. These mountains harbor the greatest diversity of conifers on the planet with 38 species.

Kalmiopsis Wilderness

OREGON

LOCATION: Rogue River-Siskiyou National Forest west of Cave Junction

LENGTH: 4 miles out and back, or longer

ELEVATION: 5,098 feet at top; 3,800 feet at trailhead

DIFFICULTY: strenuous

HIGHLIGHTS: unusual plant life, starkly beautiful burned landscape

A little-known gem of exotic quality and vast proportions, the Kalmiopsis Wilderness in southwestern Oregon is a harsh range of rocky ridgelines, forbidding canyons, and outcrops of colorfully mixed minerals metamorphosed from rock formed undersea and then pushed up by powerful tectonic forces. With stark evidence of massive wildfires in recent years, the Siskiyou Mountains here resemble no other range.

But let's be clear: this place is not for everyone. In addition to steep gradient, deadfall from recent fires riddles some paths, brushy chaparral encroaches at its will, backlogs for trail maintenance are the norm, summers heat up intensely, and, perhaps most important, water sources are widely spaced and sometimes unreliable, making dehydration a hazard. Not to freak out the ophidiophobic, but rattlesnakes also live here. Keep an eye on the trail and use extra caution where brush intrudes, especially on lower slopes in summer. Expect few people, which may be a tempting draw to some.

Broiling summer temperatures and fearsomely hot windstorms have historically combined to breed wildfires, creating a mosaic of charred and unburned forest—a harsh but beautiful landscape with unobstructed views to a mountain vastness of both black and bleached snags, regreened chaparral, and surviving forest featuring charismatic wind-sculpted conifers clinging for centuries to ridgelines that are less fire prone. The Siskiyou Mountain Club heroically clears trail here, and deserves a lot of support, but it's prudent to expect complications.

Spring is inviting when higher ranges, such as the Cascades, remain encrusted in snow. Water supplies are scarce in sizzling summer, so hike elsewhere then. Autumn is glorious, but dryness lingers.

A dramatic horn of volcanic rock rises from the recovering forest of Jeffrey pines and other emerging growth after fires swept through the Kalmiopsis Wilderness.

Winter can offer snow-free trails and springlike interludes, but watch the forecast; pounding rainstorms or surprise whiteouts can paralyze and pose dangers as severe as in higher mountains.

Yet, for all those challenges, here lies an unmatched opportunity to hike through a burned landscape that has ironically turned visually stunning in a spaciously emancipating way. Kalmiopsis Wilderness is a geographic art form of botanical wonders, fire-shaped succession, and geologic curiosity unrepeated in America. Appealing to the ecologically inquisitive, the diversity of plant life owes to a mix of ultramafic and serpentine soils, linkage to other mountain ranges, and fire adaptations—the 180,000-acre wilderness is an outsized laboratory of fire and forest relationships. Additional wildlands at its fringe should likewise be protected, as wilderness visionary Bob Marshall advocated a century ago for these mountains.

A trail complex looping 40 miles rings the bewildering topography, though not all the essential segments are walkable at this time. Check with the Forest Service or Siskiyou Mountain Club for current trail conditions. Hearty hikers in spring or fall might consider the following route. Start from the east side of the wilderness at the Onion Camp Trailhead. Hike the Kalmiopsis Rim Trail 10 miles north, skirting Whetstone Butte's prominent profile, cresting Eagle Mountain, dipping to Chetco Pass and its rutted miners' road, and then continuing up to Pearsoll Peak's inactive fire tower on the highest summit in the Kalmiopsis subrange of the Siskiyou Mountains. This route offers rare exposure with starkly burned views and it wanders among gnarled trees that have endured for ages. Other than a few barely lingering snowbanks in May, I found water only a quarter mile northeast of Chetco Pass, near the base of Pearsoll's 1,500-foot ascent.

To get there from Highway 199 in Cave Junction, drive north 4 miles, turn west at Eight Dollar Mountain Road, go 3 miles, and bear left across the Illinois River bridge. Continue up the gravel road for 12 miles to the Babyfoot Lake junction and stay right for another half mile to the Onion Camp Trailhead. The Kalmiopsis Rim Trail lies to the left of the obvious two-track that continues deceptively for only a short distance beyond the parking lot.

For another Kalmiopsis option, arrive from the west, out of Brookings. A 2-mile climb summits Vulcan Peak with views to the chaotic mélange of peaks and canyons among the recent burns of 2002 and 2017. To reach this trailhead from the Oregon coast, take Highway 101 to Brookings, turn east on North Bank Chetco River Road, go 16 miles, and turn right on the gravel South Fork Road (Forest

The summit of Vulcan Peak opens to expansive views across the Kalmiopsis Wilderness and its myriad peaks shading deep canyons of the Chetco and Illinois Rivers. A heavy April snowstorm blankets this range, which is better known for sizzling summer temperatures, though it also offers splendid spring and autumn weather.

Road 1909), which may get a bit rough. In about 10 miles, turn right on spur 261, and after another 0.2 miles, stay left for Forest Service Trail 1120 to the summit. Before reaching the trailhead, you can instead bear right on the Chetco Divide Trail (1210) and walk 5 miles to 4,667-foot Chetco Peak, which offers views from burned ridgetops. For anywhere on the Kalmiopsis Rim Trail, carry water.

The warm light of sunrise illuminates the Kalmiopsis Wilderness with its rare, fire-adapted plant life and starkly beautiful open views in southern Oregon.

Lower Rogue River Trail

LOCATION: Rogue River-Siskiyou National Forest west of Grants Pass

LENGTH: 40 miles one way, with out-and-back sections possible

ELEVATION: 700 feet at upper trailhead; 390 feet at lower trailhead

DIFFICULTY: easy to moderate

HIGHLIGHTS: riverfront hike, forest diversity, trans-Siskiyou trail

The Lower Rogue River Trail is the best footpath that transects the apex of the Klamath-Siskiyou Mountains and, for that matter, the entire Coast Range. This wilderness sojourn of three to seven days starts where the road west of Grants Pass ends its downriver limit at Grave Creek. From there, the trail follows the north side of the legendary Rogue River to a lower trailhead near Foster Bar.

This trail is unusual in following a major river many miles through wilderness. With intermittent access to the Rogue's whitewater and pools, the path clings to steep slopes and ascends tributaries to footbridges. Campsites lie along the river or its rushing feeder streams. A rich range of plant life includes old-growth conifers and hardwoods.

The Rogue is a wildlife corridor favored by black bears; carry bear-proof canisters or hang food by counterbalance, especially in the lower 10 miles. Also be aware that this is one of the best rafting rivers in the West; in late spring through fall you'll see

Cliff faces and canyon slopes tower over Oregon's Rogue River near Rainie Falls.

OPPOSITE: Near the lower end of the Rogue River Trail, Tate Creek drops vertically to the river bottom amid lush thickets of coltsfoot.

boaters floating by or parked at riverfront camps. When hiking, I seek out small sites that are less attractive to boaters. For an out-and-back hike without shuttle requirements, I prefer the upper eastern end.

Low elevations here grow terribly hot in summer, with swimming holes as salvation. Beware of poison oak and of ticks in spring. I carry Tecnu for the oak and tweezers for the ticks. Fall hiking is ideal, as the climate here is relatively mild year-round and open to travel when higher country grows cold and white. But winter has a raw wetness and hikers need to watch weather reports to avoid storms that saturate everything.

For the upstream trailhead at Grave Creek, take I-5 north of Grants Pass to Merlin, go west on Merlin-Galice Road about 30 miles to the second Rogue River bridge, cross to the north side, and turn left to the river access and trailhead. Do not leave valuables in cars. If going the distance and needing a shuttle, inquire at the Galice Resort upstream of Grave Creek or call the Rogue River-Siskiyou National Forest for a list of professional drivers.

For the lower trailhead, take Bear Camp Road from Galice to Agness with timely directions from the Forest Service, as detours are common. Or, from the west, take Highway 101 to Gold Beach, turn east, and go up the south side of the Rogue on Jerrys Flat Road for 36 miles. Pass turnoffs for Agness and Foster Bar, and then continue another half mile and turn right to the Big Bend Trailhead.

As an add-on—or a separate trip—consider a loop with views, old-growth trees, and bubbling freshets linked to the Rogue River hike. From Marial—on the trail about two-thirds the distance between Grave Creek and Big Bend and also reachable by remote dirt roads—hike up Mule Creek Trail, traverse westward across Panther Ridge with big views, and descend Clay Hill Trail back to the Rogue farther downriver.

OLYMPIC MOUNTAINS

In northwestern Washington, the Olympic Mountains rise to 7,980 feet and extend from the Pacific Ocean eastward to Puget Sound—an upheaval with aged conifers, 19 rivers splaying radially from heights topped by Mount Olympus, and sizable though shrinking glaciers.

Among mountains along the Pacific edge, the Olympics occupy a class by themselves, rising not quite from the sea but near it and extending 80 miles inland. Far higher than all other coastal sub-ranges between Southern California and Canada, and at an intensely storm-ridden latitude, these mountains breed extreme weather, some of the world's heaviest annual snowfalls, and drenching downpours nourishing the greatest ancient rain forests on the continent. The core of the range within Olympic National Park is one of America's premier wilderness areas. However, the surrounding Olympic National Forest has been systematically logged, and adjacent industrial forest continues to be clear-cut on rapid rotation.

Some 900 miles of trails penetrate many of the peninsula's river corridors. For all their grandeur, the Olympics' moderate elevation makes them ideal for hiking without acclimatization, though wet weather can be a formidable challenge most months of the year. Summer and early fall offer the best shot at a clear day.

Hoh River Valley and Mount Olympus

LOCATION: Olympic National Park

LENGTH: 36 miles out and back, with shorter and longer options

ELEVATION: 4,300 feet at base of glaciers; 600 feet at trailhead

DIFFICULTY: easy in the Hoh River Valley, strenuous above

HIGHLIGHTS: ancient forest, glaciers

PREVIOUS SPREAD: The Olympic crest outlines the horizon with the multiple summits of Washington's Mount Olympus—the highest in the Coast Range between Canada and Southern California and one of the most extensively glaciated mountains in the United States outside Alaska.

Ann Vileisis crosses the high divide between the Hoh and Sol Duc Rivers in the heart of Olympic National Park while an unexpected snowstorm soaks the mountains in July.

At 7,980 feet, Mount Olympus is by far the highest peak in the coastal chain between Canada and the heights above Los Angeles. Though its elevation seems statistically unimpressive compared to summits of the interior West, this mountain rises only 40 miles from the ocean, so the relief exceeds that of many higher peaks elsewhere. The vertical gain is comparable, for example, to that of Grand Teton over Jackson Hole, Wyoming. And Olympic summits are decidedly more glaciated and alpine than the elevations suggest. Only Mounts Rainier and Baker in the Cascades have more glacier coverage south of Canada. With its gradient, forests, glaciers, and rock all packed together so tightly, think of Olympus as a compact version of the world's greatest mountain peaks. The amount of precipitation there—more than 200 inches annually—is the most in the contiguous states, and the wettest locations are not even monitored.

Begin this remarkable hike at the Hoh Rain Forest visitor center of Olympic National Park. For 18 miles, the popular trail, with occasional primitive campsites, wends through what is arguably the most magnificent old-growth temperate forest on the planet, replete with imposing Sitka spruce, Douglas firs, western hemlocks, western red cedars, and archaic bigleaf maples that stretch the imagination of what maples can become. All this ends at Glacier Meadows and the leading edge of the well-named Blue Glacier, ramping for 2 miles up to latticeworks of crevasses, battlefields of seracs, and, finally, gaping bergschrunds at cirques near Olympus's jagged summit.

With adequate care, hikers can venture onto firm, lower portions of the glacier, but crevasses shortly yawn, snowfields steepen, and travel must be limited to mountaineers with glacier experience, crampons, ice axes, and roped safety lines. The summit climb is among the top glacier mountaineering experiences south of Canada and should only be undertaken by skilled mountaineering parties or with guides—available in Port Angeles.

Other hiking options appeal as well. Ten miles up from the Hoh River Trailhead, the Bogachiel Peak Trail turns north and in 9 miles connects with paths running another forested 10 miles down to the Sol Duc River Trailhead. Alternate routes northward connect to Boulder Creek, the Elwha Valley, and Highway 101 in its traverse of the northern Olympic Peninsula. With a car shuttle, these point-to-point hikes to the Sol Duc and Elwha make splendid weeklong trans-Olympic tours.

From Port Angeles, take Highway 101 west and then south to Upper Hoh Road. Or, from Aberdeen, take Highway 101 north and drive up the Hoh River Valley to the visitor center at the end. Permits from the national park are required for backpacking and for the Mount Olympus summit climb.

Hurricane Ridge

LOCATION: Olympic National Park south of Port Angeles

LENGTH: 3-mile loop, with longer hikes possible

ELEVATION: 6,000 feet at top; 5,242 feet at trailhead

DIFFICULTY: easy, with strenuous options

HIGHLIGHTS: views of Mount Olympus, easy highcountry access

From Port Angeles, Hurricane Ridge Road climbs 18 miles to an upper Olympic National Park visitor center, where walkers can wander the meadows and ridgelines above timberline among summer wildflowers and enjoy views to Olympus and its neighbors on a clear day. This alpine adventure comes with little effort, and the lingering snow, big views, and access to peaks are elsewhere available to this extent only at much higher elevations in the West. Even in winter, with monumental dumps of snow, the road is generally open from Friday through Sunday; call the National Park Service for status.

From the road-end visitor center, a paved 3-mile loop gains 700 feet. Also stop at mile 14.8 of Hurricane Ridge Road for Klahhane Ridge Trail and its 5-mile round trip. Or, beyond the visitor center, continue 1.5 road miles to the busy Hurricane Hill Trailhead with views to Mount Olympus. Longer routes connect north and west.

And there are more: just before reaching the Hurricane Ridge visitor center, turn left on Obstruction Point Road, open after July 4, and ridge run 8 miles southeast to the end. There I've found the best road-accessible summer backcountry skiing in America, as north faces at this high latitude are less prone to the sun cupping that afflicts more southerly mountains. From the Grand Ridge Trailhead, the path to Elk Mountain makes a 5-mile round trip, and other trails lead east and south from the road.

The Olympic Mountains are notoriously snowbound in winter and rainy throughout shoulder seasons. In summer, watch the weather report and pick a clear day, if you can, for this stellar highcountry domain.

From Seattle, take the Bainbridge Island ferry and then drive west to Highway 101. Continue north and west to Port Angeles, and on Race Street go south, leading to Hurricane Ridge Road.

A mule deer browses at timberline near Hurricane Ridge.

OPPOSITE: The heights of Mount Olympus on the left form a backdrop to alpine terrain at Hurricane Ridge.

Quinault River

LOCATION: Olympic National Park, southwest Olympic Peninsula

LENGTH: 26 miles out and back, with longer thru-hikes possible

ELEVATION: 2,004 feet at top; 676 feet at trailhead

DIFFICULTY: easy to moderate

HIGHLIGHTS: rain forest, giant trees, riverfront

The Quinault River flows from southwestern heights of the Olympic Mountains to the Pacific, and a trail to its headwaters offers a tour of old-growth forests and rushing streams with far fewer hikers than the comparable Hoh River Trail.

The largest or "champion" individuals of several tree species grow in this valley. The trail is a two- to four-day backpack trip beginning at the Graves Creek Trailhead and gradually ascending 13 miles to Enchanted Valley with its view to snowcaps. Hikers can continue 3 steeper miles to Anderson Pass, and then down the West Fork Dosewallips River for a west-to-east transect of the Olympic Range, though the shuttle is interminably long.

Watch the summer weather forecast for a break; a sunny day in a rain forest is hard to beat.

Take Highway 101 from Aberdeen in the south or Port Angeles in the north to Lake Quinault and turn east on South Shore Road. Drive 14 miles to the Quinault River bridge, but stay right there and continue 6 miles to the Graves Creek Trailhead.

Other trails on the west slope of the Olympic Mountains lead up the Queets (there is a major ford at the outset; avoid high or rising water and go in summer only!), Bogachiel, and Sol Duc Rivers, each with their own mix of ancient trees, rain forest wonders, and connecting trails that penetrate to the heart of this range.

Thirteen miles up the Quinault River Trail, the terrain opens at Enchanted Valley, with peaks of the Olympic Mountains encircling.

Dosewallips River and Anderson Pass

LOCATION: east side of Olympic National Park, southwest of Quilcene

LENGTH: 20 miles out and back, with longer trips possible

ELEVATION: 4,464 feet at top; 600 feet at trailhead

DIFFICULTY: moderate to strenuous

HIGHLIGHTS: rushing river, rain forest, Olympic peaks

Though drier than the west side of the Olympics owing to the mountains' rain shadow, it's still dripping wet on the east side. Among a suite of rivers plunging toward Puget Sound, the Dosewallips offers a hike through its emerald landscape and up to wildflower meadows and peaks shouldering Mount Anderson and its glacier. This makes a brimful day hike or excellent backpacking expedition. Call Olympic National Park for an overnight permit. Take food canisters and precautions for black bears.

From Seattle, catch the ferry to Bainbridge Island and drive west. Go south on Highway 101 to Brinnon, turn west on Dosewallips River Road, and continue to the end. Other trails on the east side of the Olympics ascend the Skokomish, Hamma Hamma, and Duckabush Rivers.

Western hemlocks, alders, thimbleberries, and vine maples enrich the floodplain of the Dosewallips River flowing off the east side of the Olympic Mountains.

ALASKA RANGES

The symphonic crescendo of the Coast Range increases beyond mountaineers' wildest fantasies with multiple subranges where the Pacific Plate, lunging northward, directly encounters the terrain of southern Alaska with vertical results. The Saint Elias Range bordering Alaska and Canada tops out with 19,850-foot Mount Logan in Yukon—the megalithic highest mountain in Canada and second-highest peak in North America, yet elusive behind persistent screens of bad weather. Westward, the Wrangell and Chugach Ranges rise monumentally in south-central Alaska.

Unlike most great mountains of the world, these heights soar essentially from sea level. Peaks of 10,000 feet here are mere foothills. Owing to extraordinary features of rock, forest, water, ice, and tundra, every page in the DeLorme *Alaska Atlas & Gazetteer* is frameable as ornate cartographic art. Ice-age grandeur describes the highest continuous mass of mountains in North America and the world's largest nonpolar ice fields. Still a work in ascending progress, Alaska's Coast Range arcs across the Pacific to Kodiak Island, where, after 5,000 miles—starting with the Baja Peninsula in Mexico—the mountains finally dip to the sea, not emerging until their next incarnation as the east coast of Asia.

Lying north of Alaska's Coast Range and mimicking its bold arc, the Alaska Range constitutes a loose continuation of the Pacific Northwest's Cascade Mountains, curving from the center of the state to the southwest and topping out with Denali—the Northern Hemisphere's highest peak at 20,320 feet. Southwestward, the Alaska Range morphs into smoking craters of the Alaska Peninsula and hopscotches across the Pacific as the 1,600-mile-long chain of Aleutian Islands—another half-continent length of volcanic cones decked out in rock and grass where trees have not taken hold.

That leaves northern Alaska, where the Brooks Range continues roughly on the alignment of the Rockies with incomparably wild country running 700 miles from Canada to the Bering Sea. Tundra and rocky peaks weather an Arctic climate made doubly severe by elevation.

Altogether, Alaska's combined Coast, Alaska, and Brooks Ranges are among the least settled mountains in the world. Exploring them presents unique challenges to hikers, yet opportunities beckon, from the nearly convenient to the absolutely extreme.

Mount Roberts

LOCATION: Tongass National Forest above Juneau

LENGTH: 9 miles out and back, with variations

ELEVATION: 3,819 feet at top; 200 feet at trailhead; 1,760 feet at top of tram

DIFFICULTY: strenuous

HIGHLIGHTS: views to mountains, glaciers, ocean, islands

First, wait for a clear day, though, to be honest, that might not happen while you're in Juneau. With rain and clouds, not much can be seen, so don't bother. But with clear skies, mountain majesty here is a phenomenon. Ever a gamble, try May through June. Rain picks up after that and, while autumn tends to be drier in many mountain regions, here it's hopelessly wet.

The hike leaves directly from Juneau and reaches above timberline with stunning views to the crest of the Coast Range, ice-age glaciers and peaks, and equally expansive scenes across the Gastineau Channel and islands of Alaska's south-eastern archipelago.

The trail starts at the end of Juneau's 6th Street and climbs through forest for 1,600 feet to the steel girders of the sightseeing tram. To skip this aerobic workout but soggy slog, you can pay and catch the tram near the cruise ship dock at the southern end of downtown, ride up with all the other tourists, and step directly into highcountry.

Meadows, rocks quilted by heather, and summer snowfields distinctly lingering above tim-berline all await. Expect a multinational mob at the tram terminal and a host of pilgrims for a half mile above it. But following ridgelines up and up, you'll notice that the sightseers dwindle and the route opens to utterly spectacular views of mountains eastward and a wraparound panorama of island seascape in other directions.

When the snow is melting and soft, careful hikers can cross a slope that's dangerously convex in its lower end—an ice ax is advised, or required, if the snow remains hard. Then continue to views eastward to the distant Devils Paw pillars of rock pointing like a throne of mountain gods vertically above an unknown thickness of glaciers, and to a horizon of scores, if not hundreds, of peaks in a coastal mountain wilderness likely unimagined. Mountain goats and bald eagles both visited quite close on my climb, though the goats were later spooked by a helicopter's harassment.

From the base near sea level, it's 2 steep miles to the top of the tram, then another 2 or so miles to the summit. Hikers with time can continue to high-country beyond Mount Roberts, but beware: the last tram down leaves at 9:00 p.m.—even though that's still broad daylight at this latitude in mid-summer. It is available one way for a modest price from May to September.

PREVIOUS SPREAD: Seen from the flanks of Mount Roberts, Alaska's Coast Range rises to the east above Juneau. Devils Paw towers over glaciers and snowfields at the border of British Columbia.

From Mount Roberts, Stephens Passage stretches southward, with Admiralty Island in the distance.

Mount Ripinski

LOCATION: directly northwest of Haines

LENGTH: 4 miles out and back

ELEVATION: 3,599 feet at top; 500 feet at trailhead

DIFFICULTY: strenuous

HIGHLIGHTS: views to archipelago, mountains, Chilkat Inlet

This hike begins just 1.7 miles from downtown Haines and offers phenomenal views to the Takshanuk Mountains of the Alaskan coastal complex, to both the Chilkat and Chilkoot Inlets on either side of Mount Ripinski, and to multitudes of glaciated peaks at the horizon line. Save this adventure for a clear day, most likely in June, though snow cover persists.

From downtown Haines, take 2nd Avenue uphill (north), and after 0.3 miles continue straight on Young Road to the end at the Skyline Trailhead. The path soon emerges above timberline, offering spacious views almost from the get-go. A heart-thumping 3,600-foot gain in 3 miles reaches Ripinski's summit. Continue on the ridgeline to Jones Gap and Shakuseyi Peak for even better views.

Just the trip to picturesque Haines is a fine outing, done via a scenic ferryboat ride from Juneau. The Alaska/Alcan road system also connects to Haines via a 216-mile paved spur highway southward from Haines Junction.

Easily reached from the town of Haines, Mount Ripinski ramps up in stark, glaciated ridgelines.

Exit Glacier

LOCATION: Kenai Fjords National Park south of Anchorage

LENGTH: 8 miles out to the edge of the ice field and back

ELEVATION: 3,400 feet at top; 1,200 feet at trailhead

DIFFICULTY: strenuous

HIGHLIGHTS: glacier, direct access to a major ice field, ice-age grandeur

Glacier-weathered mountains—still buried in ice except for their summits—crest on the deceptively distant horizon. The vast Harding Icefield narrows to become Exit Glacier, curving downward to the left in a chaos of crevasses.

This rigorous hike offers a remarkable window to the ice ages and exposure to the chaotic tumult of Exit Glacier—one among 40 that spill from the 300-square-mile Harding Icefield into ocean-bound canyons below. Spellbinding vistas stretch out across the 20-mile-wide glacial expanse.

Imagine this ice field as a lake frozen solid to impenetrable thickness and perched high among the peaks, and Exit Glacier as a riverlike outlet plunging down mountain slopes toward sea level, only frozen and fractured deeply with crevasses that appear, from a distance, as myriad navy-blue streaks on white.

The trail first ramps through a balsam poplar forest along Exit Glacier's Resurrection River outflow, which in summer pumps high and angry with silty, glaciated runoff the color of gray paint and almost as opaque. Then the path emerges into a starkly barren rockscape scoured under the weight of ice just decades ago—a mere blink in geologic time. With a vigorous rise of 1,000 feet per mile, this trail reveals active glaciation otherwise rarely seen without an extensive approach by plane, boat, backpack, or skis.

After 4 miles, the trail ends with a magisterial view of Exit Glacier's steep upper slope and across the crevasse-riddled Harding Icefield. Nunataks—gray, pointed mountaintops protruding through the top of an unknown but deep thickness of ice—ring the perimeter of the glacial universe. This remarkable scene can be reached with a strenuous one-day hike up and back, or as an overnight with campsites enticingly near the glacier, though subject to its chill and to fearsome storms at any time of year.

Late in summer, when the snow has melted and exposed the multitude of crevasses, experienced mountaineers with crampons for traction can easily climb the glacier's convex upper incline and continue on foot or skis across the nearly flat ice field. Gaping crevasses require end-run detours, but hundreds of others are narrow enough to casually step across or bridge on skis at right angles. The tempting and otherworldly nunataks appear to be within a day's journey, but are actually many miles away. I thought I might near them with a vigorous one-day workout, but after hours of skiing, they hardly looked any closer.

The short season for travel here is summer. The rest of the year, be ready for heavy snow and perpetual storms 24 hours a day, 7 days a week, which means, quite simply, staying away. Snow can remain on the trail into July. Even then, weeks might go by without the clear weather that's needed for the lusty views. And even good weather is fickle. On the blue-sky day I set off to ski across the ice field, the sky at noon quickly became threatening with a blackening stew of low pressure; the winds accelerated and only moments later bore down with ominous force. I turned around and made tracks back toward camp. Loss of visibility, hypothermia, and crevasses are all real hazards here. Take a compass in case the clouds settle, and pack adequate gear for whatever.

The National Park Service maintains a stout emergency shelter, necessarily pinned to bedrock by fat steel cables and hefty turnbuckles, about 1 mile back down from the end of the trail. Here hikers can take shelter from hurricane-force storms, as I did after judging my veteran tent to be unworthy of the approaching atmospheric event. It was a good call; even the shelter rattled all night long.

From Seward, drive north on Highway 9 for 4 miles and then turn west on Exit Glacier Road. Continue 7 miles, and then bear left to the trailhead at the end of the road.

Center Mountain

LOCATION: Kodiak Island southwest of Kodiak

LENGTH: 20 miles out and back, or 5 miles round trip to Kashevaroff Mountain

ELEVATION: 3,366 feet at top; 20 feet at trailhead

DIFFICULTY: moderate but adventurous

HIGHLIGHTS: mountainous grasslands, wildflowers, views of Kodiak Island and the Pacific Ocean

In a world devoid of trees but brilliantly greened by grasses and shrubs, Ann Vileisis progresses toward the summit of Center Mountain on Kodiak Island while the Gulf of Alaska recedes in the background.

Though few are ever likely to journey to such a remote outpost—and clearly not an outing for everyone even if it were not so radically far out—this trip is featured as the westernmost mountain hike one might ever do in North America. It is also a way to see the Coast Range in its final manifestation across the arc of southern Alaska as it conclusively disappears into the northern Pacific Ocean.

As with other southern Alaska destinations, check the weather and be ready to delay your trip or ultimately fail in waiting for a clear day. Heavy rain and milky cloud cover obscure the views that make this hike fantastically memorable, and can also make navigation in this relatively featureless terrain troublesome. Carry a compass in case conditions deteriorate, which they are likely to do. Unlike most other mountain regions, the choice for clear weather here is late May. Rain and wind increase ominously in late September.

Owing to glaciation and the slow progression of post-ice-age forests, trees of the continent end with pioneering Sitka spruce on the northeast side of Kodiak Island. Only grass, forbs, and brush with juicy crops of multiple berry species endure on the rocky terrain that continues across this island and others westward in the Aleutian Islands. Accessible by road at the base, this hike rises to Kashevaroff Mountain's summit and then continues upward with sweeping views to America's far northwestern mountains.

Starting on Alaska's mainland at the fetching little Kenai Peninsula town of Homer, orientated seaward, board the ferryboat for a 10-hour cruise in the Gulf of Alaska to Kodiak Island. Prep for inevitably impressive ocean swells if you're prone to seasickness. From Kodiak Harbor, hitch or arrange for a 12-mile ride southwest to Womens Bay. After crossing Russian Creek and then the diminutive Panamaroff Creek inlet, look for an obscure and overgrown path angling to the southwest and soon climbing out of the brush to the ridgeline of Kashevaroff Mountain. If you luck out with local help, they might know where this route is. Or they might not.

Take precautions for brown bears—like the fabled grizzlies in the Rockies, only 600 pounds heavier. In summer, they're likely fishing for salmon near stream mouths at sea level—not unlike the start of this hike! Make noise, and you'll quickly be past the red-alert zone.

Soon the path emerges with dwarf alpine vegetation and, in summer and early fall, a brilliant palate of wildflowers, huckleberries, and crowberries as the cross-country route mounts the ridge of Kashevaroff and gains its spacious, gentle summit at 2,282 feet. This view alone is worthwhile.

Continue west and southwest on the ridgeline and ramp to high points rising cumulatively toward Center Mountain's summit at 3,366 feet. Camping is possible on benches and saddles, with fresh water in rivulets draining snowbanks. Increasingly rocky, the route to the top offers views across Kodiak's wild expanse, north to ethereal glacial and volcanic peaks in Katmai National Park and Preserve on the Alaska Peninsula, and Pacific panoramas of infinity.

Another hiking destination on Kodiak Island is Barometer Mountain, perhaps a bit less intense, with a 3,000-foot climb near the Kodiak Coast Guard Station and airport runway.

Muldrow Glacier

LOCATION: Denali National Park and Preserve

LENGTH: 12 miles out and back, with variations

ELEVATION: 3,400 feet at Muldrow Glacier; 3,722 feet at Eielson visitor center

DIFFICULTY: moderate, with significant fords

HIGHLIGHTS: views to Denali, access to Muldrow Glacier, wildlife

Hiking here offers close-up views of Denali, North America's tallest mountain, remarkably large in the view though the summit is still 35 miles away. Measured from the lowlands around it, 18,000 feet is the greatest vertical relief in the world. The Muldrow hike reaches the rock-encrusted lower limits of one of Denali's longer glaciers—30 miles from headwall to terminus—a lot of ice in the age of global warming.

All precautions must be taken regarding grizzlies; the National Park Service wisely requires bear-proof food canisters. (Before canisters were available, I was forced by an adolescent bear to pack up in a hurry and abandon camp here; fortunately the mother never showed up.) No fires are allowed, and camping must be reserved in advance. Also be

aware that there is no trail for this hike; you simply follow landforms along the route described.

Descend from the Eielson visitor center, hike down the Thorofare River gravel bars, ford the stream across multiple channels if prudent, hike south a bit, and then turn up the gravel bars of Glacier Creek and continue to the clear waters of Intermittent Creek or beyond.

To reach this hike from Highway 3 or the railroad serving Denali National Park and Preserve, take the daily shuttle school bus (reservations are encouraged) on its four-hour ride to the Eielson visitor center at mile 66 of Denali Park Road. To camp before your hike, stay on the bus for another hour to its turnaround at Wonder Lake Campground,

Golden in Alaska's midnight sunset, Denali stands as the summit of North America, seen here with a telephoto lens from near Muldrow Glacier.

OPPOSITE: With its surface overloaded in cobbles, Muldrow Glacier comes to its end. Hummocks of ice—looking like brushy hills here—become covered with rocky debris as the glacier grinds its way past Denali's flanks during the journey of 30 miles from its origin at the headwalls of the great peak. Intermittent Creek enters Glacier Creek from the left; Mount Mather, northeast of Denali, rises to the right.

and then double back to Eielson the next day to hike. Buses are likely to fill in July and August—the best times for this trip.

From Eielson, five other hiking routes lead to alternate destinations, including a 2-mile round trip on the Eielson Alpine Trail just behind the visitor center, with views to Denali. Other hikes along glacial rivers, across tundra, up ridgelines, and to minor peaks of the Alaska Range are possible from spots on the bus route to Eielson, including Primrose Ridge, Polychrome Pass, Thorofare Pass, and Toklat River. For details and timely precautions, inquire with the Park Service before your trip or when entering the park.

Sheenjek River Headwaters, Brooks Range

LOCATION: Sheenjek River, Arctic National Wildlife Refuge, northeastern Alaska

LENGTH: 2 miles or more out and back (once you get there!)

ELEVATION: 6,000 feet at top; 3,400 feet at river

DIFFICULTY: strenuous

HIGHLIGHTS: Brooks Range views, Sheenjek River, caribou

The Brooks Range is North America's northernmost mountain chain, spanning arctic Alaska for 700 miles—so extremely wild and remote that it's covered here with reluctance. The costs in money and fuel are so great that few people can, or should, go to this area, and the bush flights include risks of their own, especially in shoulder seasons and bad weather. Yet the Brooks is a major range that can hardly be ignored in any book about America's mountains.

Entirely north of timberline, this seemingly endless complex of peaks and valleys is a universe of tundra, rivers shining across spacious gravel bars, buggy and boggy wetlands, and mountains that rise in abrupt profiles blanketed in scree and loose rock. The range is almost entirely without road access or trails; flying in is the usual approach.

One of many possibilities here is the upper Sheenjek River, where hikes can be done with a drop-off and pickup by bush plane or, in my case, combined with a river trip down this waterway flowing from the Brooks' highest subrange, the Romanzof Mountains near the Canadian border.

From the gravel bar of your pilot's choice north of Double Mountain, embark to high ridgelines and summits above the braided Sheenjek River—which is armored with ice in places through August because the river freezes to its bottom in winter and then continues to freeze and accumulate ice through spring. On high slopes, caribou might be seen grazing on lichens.

Serious precautions must be taken for grizzly bears, horrible weather, bugs, and route finding in one of the wildest landscapes on earth. Hiking here is not for the inexperienced or ill prepared. Flights can be arranged through charter carriers serving Fairbanks, Fort Yukon, and Arctic Village.

Free-form walking up ridgelines overlooking the Sheenjek River leads to sweeping views northward across the arctic expanse of the Brooks Range.

OPPOSITE: Above the Sheenjek River, a single caribou grazes on lichen at a high ridge of the Romanzof Mountains—the easternmost and highest subrange of the Brooks Range.

TROPICAL ISLANDS

As a finale to this book's lineup of mountain trails, two different ranges rise from tropical islands found at opposite ends of the American domain—one in the territory of Puerto Rico, the other in Hawaii.

The Luquillo Mountains of Puerto Rico rumple up from lowland jungle to a cloud forest of Sierra palms overlooking the Atlantic Ocean. Rounded by eons of rainstorms, these mountains nourish America's only eastern tropical rain forests.

In the Pacific Ocean, five major islands constitute Hawaii, farther from the continents than any other land on earth. Here both ancient volcanoes and ongoing eruptions have built subranges varying in age from 16 million years to molten rock hardening daily. On the geologically new Big Island, volcanoes spit fiery lava that oozes down to the sea. Explosive eruptions occurred as recently as this writing in 2018. Just a short airplane hop away, the oldest Hawaiian island, Kauai, ascends with tangled greenery into the clouds. The Hawaiian climate is pleasant and hikeable all year, but less rainy from April to October.

In 2017 and 2018, all these island Edens were beset by a spate of extreme climatic and geologic events—hurricanes, volcanoes, and floods—temporarily closing some of the trails highlighted here. Check with park agencies for the current status.

La Coca Trail

LOCATION: El Yunque National Forest, eastern Puerto Rico

LENGTH: 3.6 miles out and back

ELEVATION: 1,476 feet at top; 656 feet at bottom

DIFFICULTY: moderate, slippery

HIGHLIGHTS: tropical rain forest, waterfall, endemic birds and plant life

As the easternmost and southernmost mountains in the United States, the Luquillo Central Range of Puerto Rico offers unusual hiking opportunities.

The La Coca Trailhead lies along El Yunque National Forest's main road 5.4 miles south of the visitor center; drive beyond the La Coca Falls viewpoint to a parking area on the left and walk into a lush rain forest. Thriving here are 225 native tree species that are not found growing wild anywhere on the US mainland. Every tree is likely different from any other you've ever seen. The steep trail drops to La Coca Falls and onward to the stream's confluence with Río Mameyes, one of three El Yunque rivers designated in the National Wild and Scenic Rivers System. While there, I was surprised to stumble upon a sizable endangered Puerto Rican boa—right on the trail! After challenging my passage, it eventually retreated up a tree.

Also in the national forest, the Big Tree Trail features 1,000-year-old trees—walk 2 miles out and back. And the El Yunque Trail extends 6 miles round trip to the top of El Yunque Peak. On a clear day, this trail offers views across an impenetrable forest of Sierra palms to the Atlantic Ocean, a lovely blue even from a distance. However, the Luquillo Mountains' storm-prone heights saturate with 200 inches of rain a year and are often obscured in clouds. Intense rains anywhere in this forest can drop two-and-a-half inches an hour. Winter is the time to visit, as summer is tropically hot.

Protection for El Yunque occurred before any other national forest in America when the king of Spain proclaimed this mountain enclave a preserve in 1876, before the island became a US territory. In 1903, President Theodore Roosevelt established the Luquillo Forest Reserve, later expanded to a 28,000-acre national forest—one of the nation's smallest. More acreage should be added to supplement this rare ecosystem and to protect its headwaters.

Fly from East Coast cities to San Juan, and then drive a rental car to El Yunque National Forest at the eastern part of the island. Camping is not allowed in the forest; stay in nearby towns and resorts. As of this writing, the island is still recovering from Hurricane Maria's devastating damage in 2017.

PREVIOUS SPREAD: Seen from overlooks in Kōkeʻe State Park, the Nāpali Cliffs slant radically to the Pacific Ocean on the west side of the island of Kauai—the wettest of the Hawaiian Islands.

This waterfall highlights the La Coca Trail through its tropical arboretum and steamy undergrowth on the flanks of Puerto Rico's Luquillo Mountains.

Kīlauea Crater

LOCATION: Hawaii Volcanoes National Park, island of Hawaii

LENGTH: 4-mile loop

ELEVATION: 4,000 feet at trailhead; drops 400 feet

DIFFICULTY: easy

HIGHLIGHTS: active volcanic caldera, tropical vegetation

Easily reached by road—barring eruptions—Hawaii Volcanoes National Park is the best place nationwide, and perhaps worldwide, to see active volcanic features. Hikers are able to encircle the rim of a steaming crater, considered the most active on earth. The wide, nearly flat mountaintop basin features hundreds of fumaroles and other attractions. However, severe eruptions in 2018 closed all caldera trails, and some may remain off-limits for years. With little respite, Kīlauea is considered the most likely volcano in the United States to next erupt. Check with the national park for the current status and recommended hikes.

The park has typically offered 150 miles of trails, including immersion in enchanting tree-fern forests on the east side of the Kīlauea Crater southeast of the visitor center. Before 2018, the Kīlauea Iki Trail descended 400 feet to the crater, which even then was steaming from the legacy of volcanic events in 1959.

From Hilo, drive south on Highway 11 for 28 miles and into Hawaii Volcanoes National Park (assuming the conditions allow). Turn right on Crater Rim Drive and continue to the visitor center, where you can plan your hike based on rangers' recommendations.

Active lava flows can sometimes be seen outside the national park near sea level. A popular trail at the southern end of Chain of Craters Road leads to oozing lava—flaming red and incinerating everything in its path as it pours across black rock. Hiking after sunset with a flashlight to view the molten flows is a popular local pastime. Check with Hawaii State Parks for the current status. And stay on designated trails!

Hawaii Volcanoes National Park and the lava flows on the Big Island are the best illustrations of mountains being continuously formed and re-formed through the types of volcanic and seismic phenomena that have created mountains elsewhere in America.

A path carefully marked for safety by national park rangers wends its way along the southeast side of Kīlauea Crater—a trail closed indefinitely by spectacular eruptions in 2018.

OPPOSITE: With twilight accentuating the surreal glow of molten rock, the Kamokuna lava flow nears the sea on the Big Island of Hawaii.

Nāpali Cliffs and Kalalau Beach

LOCATION: Nāpali Coast State Wilderness Park, west side of island of Kauai

LENGTH: 22 miles out and back

ELEVATION: 800 feet at top; sea level at both ends, with continuous gradient

DIFFICULTY: strenuous, long

HIGHLIGHTS: ocean views, coastal mountains, beach, waterfalls

Two miles from the Keʻe Beach Trailhead, the dicey footpath to Kalalau Beach crosses Hanakoa Stream, where a side trip can be taken upstream to a waterfall.

FOLLOWING SPREAD: The Nāpali Cliffs and Kalalau Trail begin at Hāʻena State Park, where thundering surf pounds the shores of America's westernmost mountains.

At the northwest side of the Hawaiian complex, the island of Kauai receives the most rain, watering tropical vegetation that includes myriad exotic introduced species and a treasured suite of struggling native plants. Spectacular beaches can be found and mountain hikes can be taken in several parks, but the legendary backpacking experience is the pilgrimage to Kalalau Beach.

This rigorous hike has been regarded as the top beach-destination backpack outing in America and is noted worldwide. However, in the interest of full disclosure, the route is not for novices, hiking boots are needed for unstable trail surfaces, bugs can be bad along the way, and tour-industry helicopters are an absolute plague. Stream crossings are prone to flash flooding that may require delays of a day or more. Otherwise hikers risk being washed out to sea, which has happened. The 11 miles seem like a lot more. Most trekkers need a full day or two to navigate the steep climbing, narrow tread, crumbling rock, and constantly undulating passage along the precipitous eroding coastline. The trail was closed in 2017 after the wettest rainstorm in American history dumped 50 inches in 24 hours and triggered landslides. Check with Hawaii State Parks for current conditions. All that said, this is still the Nāpali Coast, and nothing compares.

Far less ambitious than the full hike, a day hike starts at the Keʻe Beach Trailhead and runs 2 miles with a few ocean views to Hanakapiai Beach. Swimming is not recommended due to the dangerous surf, and the camp has the unfortunate reputation of being filthy. Another 4 miles lead to Hanakoa Stream and a more suitable campsite,

and 5 more miles reach the prize of Kalalau and its spacious, stunningly beautiful beach, with campsites perched in the forest above. A waterfall at the far end sprays down from junglelike Nāpali highlands onto the sand. Though tempting, do not linger there owing to falling rocks.

Winter trips here are delightfully tropical and balmy when the American mainland is locked in cold, but summer is otherwise better, with relatively drier weather and calmer seas. Purify all water and follow protocols regarding human waste at this extremely popular site. Permits for all trips except day hikes covering the first 4 miles are required from Hawaii State Parks. They are in high demand and require lead time of many months.

From the airport on Kauai, drive or catch a ride on Highway 560 around the northeastern shore to the island's northwest side at Hāʻena State Park. It is not a good idea to leave vehicles at the trailhead overnight, as pried-open trunks of rental cars attest; park farther back in the state park and return by foot to the trailhead or otherwise arrange for your pickup.

Rounding out this experience, or standing in for it, views of the Nāpali Cliffs are more clearly seen from an entirely different highway that leads to the top, with short walks and also the Awaʻawapuhi Trail—a strenuous 7-mile round trip at Kōkeʻe State Park. From Waimea, take Highway 552 or 550 to Kōkeʻe.

Slanting dramatically down into the Pacific Ocean, these westernmost slopes of the United States make a good conclusion to a tour of mountains in America.

The Quest for Beauty and Adventure

WE ALL HAVE OUR OWN REASONS for hiking on mountain trails and seeking what they offer. For me, the top motivators are beauty and adventure. I hike in order to see. Not to say that the sound of bubbling streams, the smell of springtime, the feel of rock underfoot, and the companionship of good friends are not important. But the scene is what propels me outward and onward, whether on an afternoon stroll or a backpacking trip of epic proportions. To be immersed in beauty is the goal. Beauty reigns among mountains that rise unscathed—or only lightly touched—by the gears and the wires, the pavement and the trash, the noise and the clutter of the industrial and technological ages.

No less motivating than beauty, the quest for adventure offers an escape from the mundane and arrival at a place where one can seek rewards that stir the body, mind, and spirit. The pursuit of both beauty and adventure has driven my visits to mountain destinations across America ever since my earliest trips to mountains began.

Among the hikes featured here, the first one I explored was the Youghiogheny Loop at Ohiopyle State Park in Pennsylvania. In the late 1700s, my ancestors moved to that splendid bend along the quintessentially Appalachian river. Each summer my family returned to visit relatives, and my father took me on the hike that I describe in this book.

The excitement of being in real mountains—and not just the Appalachian foothills where we lived—thrilled me beyond words. The green canopy of maples, ashes, and oaks seemed skyscraping. Hemlock roots gripped for life over sandstone slabs and on top of cliffs that begged to be climbed. The river's white foam refreshed with its plunging route that tempted me to escape, bend after bend, into the great unknown. The crest of Chestnut Ridge, looming above, had been sculpted and trimmed for eons by the winding path of the river and stood high in the steamy summer atmosphere.

I've returned many times to that formative mountain stronghold. While nature in other places has been diminished, that trail—and the window it opened to beauty and adventure—remains intact. In fact, the trees are double the girth I knew as a child, the water flows cleaner now that coal-mine acid has been checked, and a stream of smiling people tread the footpath that decades ago was scarcely used.

While that mountain hike has remained a touchstone for my lifetime, one of the most recent hikes I've enjoyed was on Mount Baker, a continent away in northern Washington. For years that snow-cone peak, iced by glaciers that crunch downward toward emerald forests, had lured me near. But opaque banks of clouds and repelling rain or snow had perpetually hung like a curtain that never opened for the show to begin. And then, when I happened to be canoeing on the Skagit River nearby, the forecast sounded good.

My wife, Ann, and I began the drive before dawn and arrived at the trailhead while the sun edged up from the horizon. After packing a lunch and essential gear, we started up the trail toward Mount Baker's glacial northern slope. The monolithic volcano seemed to expand as we crossed meadows and ridgelines that grew more exposed, the views opening to a summit that loomed bigger than life in front of us. We touched the ice's edge near a jumble of crevasses where seracs, as house-sized blocks of ice, had been stacked by the glacier's downward push.

While the afternoon wore on, clouds began to coalesce, and then they darkened with blue-gray underbellies and the wind picked up. We hustled back down the trail, and after cooking dinner on our camp stove, we fell asleep in our van as the night grew black.

Ten hours later, at first light, I heard the crisp static of windblown snowflakes stinging our walls. Out the window I saw the first few inches of white already covering the ground, so I wasted no time rolling back down the fabled mountain to snow line among the dripping ferns and cedars of the Nooksack River. It snowed six feet that day in the highcountry, and the trail we had followed remained covered until the next summer.

I now remember those two hikes—the Appalachians' Youghiogheny at the beginning of my lifelong passion for mountains and the Cascade Range's Mount Baker much later—as bookends to all the outings featured

here. Some trails call like neighbors close to home; others appeal from far away. Some are found with a stroll and others on expeditions lasting days or weeks. Make your own choices among these 100 trails and countless others wherever mountains rise.

Mount Heyburn rises from Fourth Bench Lake in the Sawtooth Mountains of Idaho.

Suggested Reading List

Guidebooks to mountain trails can be found online by searching for virtually any mountain range, state, national park, or national forest. Good sources are too many to list here, though all offer interesting and useful details, with combined coverage of thousands of trails nationwide. In addition, websites offer information on nearly all of America's popular hiking destinations; simply search by name. Natural history guidebooks also interpret the environment of many ranges. *Backpacker Magazine* likewise has a decades-long archive of excellent articles, and every issue includes tips on where to go.

Given that specific guidebooks or instructions are easy to find, I'll list, instead, some titles that I consider classics of mountain lore, covering not the details of where to go but rather the backstory of mountain fascination and understanding. Consider this list a brief introduction to a topic that sprawls across the continent, the ages, and the variable genres of literature, science, and narrative.

Arno, Stephen F., and Ramona P. Hammerly. *Timberline: Mountain and Arctic Forest Frontiers.*
A description of trees and biological processes of the highcountry.

Beckey, Fred. *Mountains of North America: The Great Peaks and Ranges of the Continent.*
A notorious mountaineer's reflections on legendary peaks.

Berger, Karen, and Bart Smith. *America's Great Hiking Trails.*
Narratives on America's officially designated national scenic trails.

Brooks, Maurice. *The Appalachians.*
The standard natural history of America's oldest and most populated range.

Farb, Peter. *The Face of North America: The Natural History of a Continent.*
A classic geography of the continent written for the general reader.

Jerome, John. *On Mountains: Thinking about Terrain.*
A collection of fine essays on the topic of mountains.

Jorgensen, Neil. *A Guide to New England's Landscape.*
A guide to the natural processes forming the mountains of the Northeast.

Kauffmann, John M. *Alaska's Brooks Range: The Ultimate Mountains.*
A survey of America's northernmost mountains.

King, Brian. *The Appalachian Trail: Celebrating America's Hiking Trail.*
A definitive history and celebration of the Appalachian Trail.

Larabee, Mark, and Barney Scout Mann. *The Pacific Crest Trail: Exploring America's Wilderness Trail.*
A definitive history and celebration of the Pacific Crest Trail.

McNamee, Gregory, ed. *The Mountain World: A Literary Celebration.*
An anthology of mountain-inspired literature.

McPhee, John. *Annals of the Former World: Basin and Range* (Book 1) and *Rising from the Plains* (Book 3).
A journalist's investigation of the geology of the Rockies and the Desert Ranges.

The Mountaineers. *Mountaineering: The Freedom of the Hills.*
The bedrock reference book on technique and mountain travel, good for hikers as well as climbers.

Muir, John. *The Mountains of California.*
A mountain-centric volume by America's first great wildlands preservationist and the father of mountain literature.

Palmer, Tim. *Luminous Mountains: The Sierra Nevada of California.*
My own endeavor to capture the nature and magic of this extraordinary range.

Palmer, Tim. *Pacific High: Adventures in the Coast Ranges from Baja to Alaska.*
A narrative of informed travel through the mountains of the West Coast.

Price, Larry W. *Mountains and Man: A Study of Process and Environment.*
The standard mountain geography book.

Wolfe, Art. *Seven Summits: The High Peaks of the Pacific Northwest.*
Stunning photography of the Northwest's highest peaks, featuring aerial scenes.

Zwinger, Ann. *Beyond the Aspen Grove.*
A narrative guide to the Rocky Mountains.

About the Photographs

For many years I used a Canon A-1 camera with 17-200mm FD lenses, but most of the photos here were taken with a Canon 5D digital camera with 17-200mm L-series zoom lenses and a 50mm L-series lens. For adventures when a small kit was needed, I carried a Fujifilm digital X-E2 with its 18-55mm and 55-200mm XF zoom lenses.

With the goal of showing landscapes as accurately and realistically as possible, I limit myself to minor postphoto adjustments for contrast and color under Apple's basic photo program. I use no artificial light or filters, and do nothing to alter the content of the photos. The overriding principle of my work is to share with others the beauty and adventures that I've been privileged to see and experience in the natural world and in traveling mountains nationwide.

The deep green of the forest begins to turn with the first trace of autumn color along the Appalachian Trail on Connecticut's Bear Mountain.

Acknowledgments

Every step of the way, my wife, Ann Vileisis, has been a part of this book. She provided ideas, inspiration, encouragement, reviews, photo modeling, logistical support, and the absolute best of hiking and backpacking companionship. Her time away from her own accomplished writing career and her inspired work to protect the wild places where we live on the coast of southern Oregon will forever be appreciated.

Associate publisher Jim Muschett at Rizzoli saw the potential for this book at the outset, and it was a pleasure working with the entire professional team he assembled: the extremely capable editor Candice Fehrman, the brilliant designer Susi Oberhelman, and the dedicated publicist Jessica Napp.

The endpaper map for this book was produced by Cartagram's Steven Gordon—not only a fine cartographer but also an artist who was eager to create exactly what was needed.

For logistical help, including rides to trailheads, pickups late in the day, overnight lodging, tips about where to go, belays on glaciers, and moral support, thanks to Bob Banks, Greg and Mary Bettencourt, Tinelle Bustam, Ken Cline, Don Elder, Peter and Linda Enticknap, John Helland, Andre Pessis, Jeff Pflueger, Steve Schmitz, Nick Shema, and Vibeke Wilberg.

For reviews of selected trail descriptions, thanks to Greg Bettencourt, Tinelle Bustam, Ken Cline, Gary Felsman, Pat Ford, Kristine Johnson, Andy Kerr, Al Kesselheim, Michael Lane, Char Miller, Jeff Parker, Steve Schmitz, Nick Shema, Kobee Stalder, Wayne Steinmetz, Barbara Timock, and others.

For the original seeds, the fertile ground for germination, and the nourishment to explore, learn, care, and share with others, my parents, Jane and Jim Palmer, could not have done better.

The Uinta Mountains of Utah tower over lodgepole pines and aspens along the trail to Amethyst Lake and Ostler Peak.

First published in the United States of America in 2019 by Rizzoli International Publications, Inc.

300 Park Avenue South   •   New York, NY 10010   •   www.rizzoliusa.com

Publisher: Charles Miers   •   Associate Publisher: James Muschett   •   Managing Editor: Lynn Scrabis   •   Editor: Candice Fehrman
Design: Susi Oberhelman   •   Endpaper Map: Steven Gordon, Cartagram

Printed in China

2019 2020 2021 2022 / 10 9 8 7 6 5 4 3 2 1

ISBN-13: 978-0-8478-6542-0   •   Library of Congress Catalog Control Number: 2019930135

Visit us online:

Facebook.com/RizzoliNewYork   •   Twitter: @Rizzoli_Books   •   Instagram.com/RizzoliBooks   •   Pinterest.com/RizzoliBooks
Youtube.com/user/RizzoliNY   •   Issuu.com/Rizzoli

CAPTIONS FOR PHOTOS ON THE OPENING PAGES OF THIS BOOK:
ABOVE: A marmot poses along the Ramparts Trail at Spectra Point in Cedar Breaks National Monument in Utah.
PAGE 1: Heights of the Sierra reach their maximums toward the southern end of the range. Here Ann Vileisis treks westward from Cottonwood Lakes.
PAGES 2–3: Early autumn snowfall dusts the highest peaks of the North Cascades in Washington near the Canadian border. **PAGES 4–5:** The West Branch of
Double Run tumbles over waterfalls and through bedrock chutes seen from the Link Trail, which adjoins the Loyalsock Trail in a network of
hiking paths through Worlds End State Park in Pennsylvania. **PAGES 6–7:** Titcomb Basin's austere beauty highlights the Wind River Range in Wyoming.